Contents

What is Databricks

Databricks is a unified set of tools for building, deploying, sharing, and maintaining enterprise-grade data solutions at scale. The Databrick Lakehouse platform integrates with cloud storage for creating and deploying the cloud infrastructure associated with Databrick workspace.

Databricks is primarily used to:
- Build and deploy data engineering workflows, machine learning models, analytics dashboards, and more.
- Process, store, clean, share, analyse, model, and monetize the datasets with solutions from BI to generative AI.

The Azure Databricks workspace provides a unified interface and tools for most data tasks, including:

- Data processing workflows scheduling and management
- Generating dashboards and visualizations
- Managing security, governance, high availability, and disaster recovery
- Data discovery, annotation, and exploration
- Machine learning (ML) modeling, tracking, and model serving
- Generative AI solutions

In addition to the workspace UI, user can interact with Azure Databricks programmatically with the following tools:
- REST API
- CLI
- Terraform

User can create Azure Databrick workspace from Azure portal. The integration is needed between the Azure Databrick workspace and cloud account. User can configure this integration. Azure Databricks deploys compute clusters in the user's cloud account to process data. Data is stored in cloud object storage. The compute cluster consists of Virtual machines which are provisioned in user's cloud account.

Use cases for Azure Databricks

The following use cases highlight how organization can leverage Azure Databricks to accomplish tasks essential to processing, storing, and analysing the data that drives critical business functions and decisions.

Build an enterprise data Lakehouse

The Data Lakehouse combines the strengths of enterprise data warehouses and data lakes to accelerate, simplify, and unify enterprise data solutions. The Databricks Lakehouse combines the

ACID transactions and data governance of enterprise data warehouses with the flexibility and cost-efficiency of data lakes. The Databricks Lakehouse keeps data in massively scalable cloud object storage. The primary components of the Databricks Lakehouse are Delta tables & Unity Catalog. Delta Lake is an optimized storage layer that supports ACID transactions and schema enforcement. Unity Catalog is a unified, fine-grained governance solution for data and AI. Delta lake & Unity Catalog will be covered in detail in later part of the book.

Data Lakehouse often use a data design pattern that incrementally improves, enriches, and refines data as it moves through layers of staging and transformation. Data Lakehouse enables business intelligence (BI) and machine learning (ML) on all data. Data engineers, data scientists, analysts, and production systems can all use the data lakehouse as their single source of truth.

ETL and Data Engineering

Databricks combines the power of Apache Spark with Delta Lake and custom tools to provide an ETL (extract, transform, load) pipeline. Data engineering provides data that is available, clean, and stored in data models. User can use SQL, Python, and Scala to compose ETL logic and then orchestrate scheduled job deployment.

Databricks provides a number of custom tools for data ingestion, including Auto Loader, an efficient and scalable tool for incrementally loading data from cloud object storage and data lakes into the data lakehouse.

Machine learning, AI, and Data science

Databricks machine learning provides a suite of tools tailored to the needs of data scientists and ML engineers, including MLflow and the Databricks Runtime for Machine Learning.

Data warehousing, Analytics, and BI

Databricks provide a powerful platform for running analytic queries. Administrators configure scalable compute clusters as SQL warehouses, allowing end users to execute complex queries. Users can run queries against data in the lakehouse using the SQL query editor or in notebooks.

Large language models and generative AI

Databricks Runtime for Machine Learning includes libraries like Hugging Face Transformers that allow us to integrate existing pre-trained models into the workflow.

With Databricks, user can customize a LLM on data for a specific task. With the support of open-source tooling, such as Hugging Face and DeepSpeed, user can efficiently take a foundation LLM and start training with their own data to have more accuracy for domain and workload.

Data governance

Unity Catalog provides a unified data governance model for the Data Lakehouse. Access control permissions are configured for Unity Catalog. Databricks administrators can manage permissions for teams and individuals. Privileges are managed with access control lists (ACLs) through UIs or SQL syntax. The lakehouse makes data sharing within organization as simple as granting query access to a table or view. For sharing outside of secure environment, Unity Catalog features a managed version of Delta Sharing.

DevOps, CI/CD, and task orchestration

Databrick provides tools for versioning, automating, scheduling, deploying code and production resources. It simplifies monitoring, orchestration, and operations. Databrick Workflows schedule Azure Databricks notebooks, SQL queries, and other arbitrary code. Repos let user sync Azure Databricks projects with a number of popular git providers like GitHub Enterprise, Bitbucket Server, Azure DevOps Server, and GitLab.

Real-time and streaming analytics

Azure Databricks leverages Apache Spark Structured Streaming to work with streaming data and incremental data changes. Structured Streaming integrates tightly with Delta Lake. These technologies provide the foundations for both Delta Live Tables and Auto Loader. These topics will be covered in later part of the book.

Databricks Lakehouse

A data Lakehouse is a new, open data management architecture that combines the flexibility, cost-efficiency, and scale of Data Lake and ACID transactions of data warehouses. It enables business intelligence (BI) and machine learning (ML) on all data.

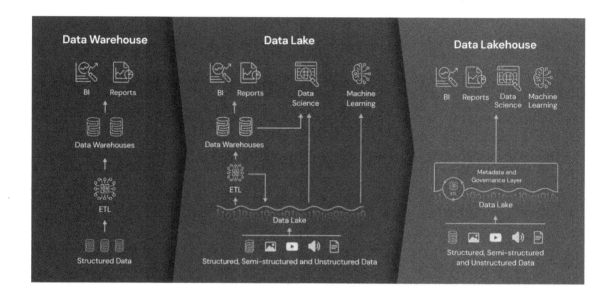

Data Lakehouses are enabled by combining data structures and data management features of Data warehouse and low-cost storage used for Data lakes. Merging data warehouse & Data lakes together into a single system helps move data team faster. Data Lakehouse also ensures that teams have the most complete and up-to-date data available for data science, machine learning, and business analytics projects.

As can be seen from the above image, Business intelligence (BI) and Machine learning (ML) using Data Lake required both Data warehouse and Data lake. This increases complexity in case of using just Data Lake.

Lakehouse provides the following key features:

- Transaction support: - It provides ACID support which ensures consistency as multiple users concurrently read or write data. Lakehouse uses Delta Lake and builds upon the ACID guarantees provided by the open-source Delta Lake protocol. ACID stands for atomicity, consistency, isolation, and durability.
- Schema enforcement and governance: - The Lakehouse support schema enforcement and evolution.
- BI support: Lakehouse enable using BI tools directly on the source data. This reduces staleness and reduces latency,

- Storage is decoupled from compute: - Storage and compute are separated. Thus, these systems can scale to many more concurrent users and larger data sizes.
- Openness: - The storage formats used are open and standardized, such as parquet. Databrick Lakehouse provide an API so that data can be accessed directly from applications.
- Support for unstructured to structured data: - The Lakehouse can be used to store, refine, analyse, and access data types needed for many new data applications. Data can be images, video, audio, semi-structured data, and text.
- End-to-end streaming: - It support streaming, and this eliminates the need for separate systems dedicated to serving real-time data applications.

Lakehouse Delta Lake transactions use log files stored alongside data files to provide ACID guarantees at a table level. Because the data and log files backing Delta Lake tables live together in cloud object storage, reading and writing data can occur simultaneously without risk of many queries resulting in performance degradation or deadlock. All requests will connect to the same single copy of the data, and they will receive the most current version of the data at the time of query execution.

Medallion Lakehouse Architecture

The architecture provides a multi-layered approach to building a single source of truth. This architecture guarantees atomicity, consistency, isolation, and durability as data passes through multiple layers of validations and transformations before being stored in a layout optimized for efficient analytics. The terms bronze (raw), silver (validated), and gold (enriched) describe the quality of the data in each of these layers.

Medallion architecture does not replace other dimensional modelling techniques. Schemas and tables within each layer can take on a variety of forms and degrees of normalization depending on the frequency and nature of data updates and the downstream use cases for the data.

Bronze layer

The bronze layer contains raw unvalidated data. Data ingested in the bronze layer typically:
- Maintains the raw state of the data source.
- Is appended incrementally and grows over time.
- Can be any combination of streaming and batch transactions.

Retaining the full, unprocessed history of each dataset provides us the ability to recreate any state of a given data system.

Silver Layer

The silver layer represents a validated, deduplicated & enriched version of data that can be trusted for downstream analytics. Implementing a silver layer efficiently will immediately unlock many of the potential benefits of the Lakehouse.

Gold Layer

Gold data is often highly refined and aggregated, containing data that powers analytics, machine learning, and production applications. Gold tables represent data that has been transformed into knowledge, rather than just information. Gold tables are often stored in a separate storage container.

Aggregations, joins, and filtering are handled before data is written to the gold layer. So, users should see low latency query performance while retrieving data from gold tables.

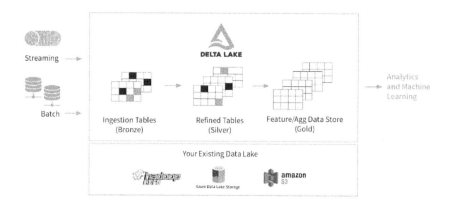

Data objects in the Databricks Lakehouse

The Databricks Lakehouse organizes data stored with Delta Lake in cloud object storage with familiar relations like database, tables, and views. This model combines many of the benefits of an enterprise data warehouse with the scalability and flexibility of a data lake.

The Databricks Lakehouse architecture combines data stored with the Delta Lake protocol in cloud object storage with metadata registered to a metastore. The metastore contains all of the metadata that defines data objects in the lakehouse.

There are five primary objects in the Databricks Lakehouse.

- Catalog: A grouping of databases. Every database is associated with a catalog.
- Database or schema: A grouping of objects in a catalog. Databases contain tables, views, and functions.
- Table: A collection of rows and columns stored as data files in object storage.
- View: A saved query typically against one or more tables or data sources. Creating a view does not process or write any data. Only the query text is registered to the metastore in the associated database. Query is executed when view is invoked.
- Function: Functions allow user to associate user-defined logic with a database. Functions can return either scalar values or sets of rows.

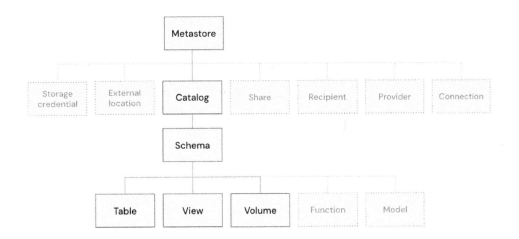

Databricks architecture

Databricks is structured to enable secure cross-functional team collaboration. Many backend services are managed by Databricks. Databricks operates out of a control plane and a data plane.

- The control plane includes the backend services that Databricks manages. Notebook commands and many other workspace configurations are stored in the control plane and encrypted at rest.
- User's cloud account manages the data plane where data resides. This is also where data is processed. Below is the most common architecture for Databricks.

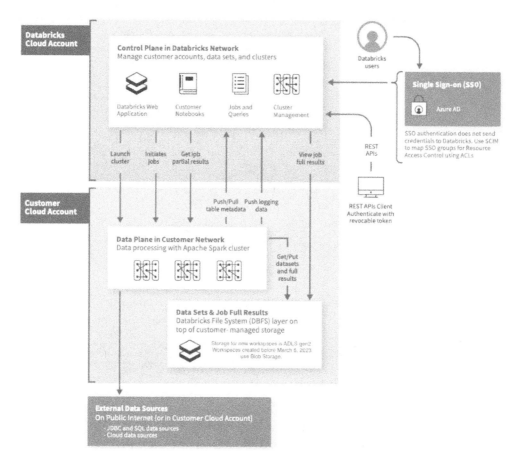

Architectures can vary depending on custom configurations like associating a virtual network with Azure Databrick workspace for enhanced security.

Data is stored at rest in cloud account in the data plane and in users' own data sources. It is not stored in the control plane. This helps maintaining control and ownership of data.

Interactive notebook results are stored in a combination of the control plane (partial results for presentation in the UI) and cloud storage. If user wants interactive notebook results stored only in cloud account storage, *interactive notebook results in the customer account* for workspace need to be enabled. This can be done by asking Databricks representative.

Load data

Databricks offers a variety of ways to load data into a Lakehouse backed by Delta Lake. The different ways of loading data are Auto Loader, Delta Live Table, COPY INTO, external sources etc.

Auto Loader

Auto Loader incrementally processes new data files as they arrive in cloud storage. Auto Loader can load data files from AWS S3, Azure Data Lake Storage Gen2 (ADLS Gen2), Google Cloud Storage, Azure Blob Storage, and Databricks File System (DBFS, dbfs:/). Auto Loader can ingest JSON, CSV, PARQUET, AVRO, ORC, TEXT, and BINARYFILE file formats.

Auto Loader provides a Structured Streaming source called *cloudFiles*. Given an input directory path on the cloud file storage, the *cloudFiles* source automatically processes new files as they arrive, with the option of also processing existing files in that directory. Auto Loader has support for both Python and SQL in Delta Live Tables.

Auto Loader can be used to process billions of files to migrate or backfill a table. Auto Loader scales to support near real-time ingestion of millions of files per hour. Auto loader ensures that data is processed exactly once. It uses checkpoint location to store the information of data processed. In case of failures, Auto Loader can resume from where it left off by information stored in the checkpoint location and continue to provide exactly-once guarantees when writing data into Delta Lake. User don't need to maintain or manage any state to achieve fault tolerance or exactly once semantics.

Databricks recommends Auto Loader whenever user uses Apache Spark Structured Streaming to ingest data from cloud object storage. APIs are available in Python and Scala.

In Apache Spark, files can be read incrementally using: -

spark.readStream.format(fileFormat).load(directory)

```
df = spark.readStream.format("cloudFiles") \
.option("cloudFiles.format", "csv") \
.option("header", "true") \
.schema(<schema>) \ # provide a schema here for the files
.load(<path>)
```

If the path contains many other files format then use pathGlobfilter for filtering only those files e.g., if user would like to parse only csv files in a directory that contains files with different suffixes, user can do:

```
df = spark.readStream.format("cloudFiles") \
.option("cloudFiles.format", "csv") \
.option("pathGlobfilter", "*.csv")
.option("header", "true") \
.schema(<schema>) \ # provide a schema here for the files
.load(<path>)
```

When user knows schema, but wants to know whenever user receives unexpected data, Databricks recommends using the rescuedDataColumn. It will collect all new fields as well as data type mismatches in _rescued_data.

```
df = spark.readStream.format("cloudFiles") \
.option("cloudFiles.format", "csv") \
.option("header", "true") \
.option("rescuedDataColumn", "_rescued_data") \ # makes sure that you don't lose data
.schema(<schema>) \ # provide a schema here for the files
.load(<path>)
```

Auto Loader can be used with Unity Catalog. User can use Auto Loader to ingest data from any external location managed by Unity Catalog. User must have READ FILES permissions on the external location. Unity Catalog will be covered in later sections.

In the below example, the json data is read from cloud storage and added to Unity catalog table(dev_table). The table dev_table is contained in dev_database database which in turn is contained within dev_catalog catalog.

```
checkpoint_path = "abfss://dev-bucket@<storage-account>.dfs.core.windows.net/_checkpoint/dev_table"

(spark.readStream
    .format("cloudFiles")
    .option("cloudFiles.format", "json")
    .option("cloudFiles.schemaLocation", checkpoint_path)
    .load("abfss://autoloader-source@<storage-account>.dfs.core.windows.net/json-data")
    .writeStream
    .option("checkpointLocation", checkpoint_path)
    .trigger(availableNow=True)
    .toTable("dev_catalog.dev_database.dev_table"))
```

Auto Loader provides the following benefits over using Structured Streaming on file source:

- *Scalability*: Auto Loader can discover billions of files efficiently. Backfills can be performed asynchronously.
- *Performance*: The cost of discovering files with Auto Loader scales with the number of files that are being ingested.
- *Schema inference and evolution support*: Auto Loader can detect schema drifts. It can notify user when schema changes happen and rescue data.

- Auto Loader can automatically set up file notification services on storage to make file discovery much cheaper.

External Data

Databricks has built-in keyword bindings for all the data formats natively supported by Apache Spark. Databricks uses Delta Lake as the default protocol for reading and writing data and tables, whereas Apache Spark uses Parquet.

The following data formats can be used in Databrick:

- Delta Lake
- Delta Sharing
- Parquet
- ORC
- JSON
- CSV
- Avro
- Text
- Binary

Delta Live Tables

Delta Live Tables is a declarative framework for building reliable, maintainable, and testable data processing pipelines. Delta Live Tables manages task orchestration, cluster management, monitoring, data quality, and error handling. Users define the transformations to perform on data.

In Delta Live Tables pipeline, streaming tables and materialized views are defined. Delta Live Tables transforms data based on queries defined for each processing step. Data quality is enforced using Delta Live Tables expectations, which allow to define expected data quality and specify how to handle records that fail those expectations.

Delta Live Tables datasets are the streaming tables, materialized views, and views.

Delta Live Tables datasets

Streaming table

A streaming table is a Delta table which supports streaming or incremental data processing. Streaming tables allow to process a growing dataset, handling each row only once. Streaming tables are good for most ingestion workloads because most datasets grow continuously over time. Streaming tables provides data freshness and low latency. Streaming table is quite useful for massive scale transformations, as results can be incrementally calculated as new data arrives, keeping results up to date without needing to fully recompute all source data with each update. Streaming tables are designed for data sources that are append-only.

Materialized view

A materialized view (or live table) is a view where the results have been precomputed. Materialized views are powerful because they can handle any changes in the input. Each time the pipeline executes, query results are recalculated to reflect changes in source datasets. Delta Live Tables implements materialized views as Delta tables.

Views

Views in Azure Databricks compute results from source datasets as they are queried. It leverages caching optimization. Delta Live Tables does not publish views to the catalog, so views can be referenced only within the pipeline in which they are defined. Views are useful as intermediate queries. Databricks recommends using views to enforce data quality constraints, transform and enrich datasets.

Dataset type	How are records processed through defined queries?
Streaming table	Each record is processed exactly once. This assumes an append-only source.
Materialized views	Records are processed as required to return accurate results for the current data state. Materialized views should be used for data

	sources with updates, deletions, or aggregations, and for change data capture processing (CDC).
Views	Records are processed each time the view is queried. Use views for intermediate transformations and data quality checks that should not be published to public datasets

SQL syntax can be used to declare a dataset with Delta Live Tables. Databricks recommends Delta Live Tables with SQL as the preferred way for SQL users to build new ETL, ingestion, and transformation pipelines. It allows users to declare dependencies between datasets. This ensures that updates occur in the correct order.

User can use notebooks or SQL files to write Delta Live Tables SQL queries. The below code declares a Delta Live Tables pipeline on a dataset containing Wikipedia clickstream data to:

- Read the raw JSON clickstream data into a raw data table.
- Read the records from the raw data table and use Delta Live Tables expectations to create a new table that contains cleansed data.
- Use the records from the cleansed data table to make Delta Live Tables queries that create derived datasets.

The following example creates a table by loading data from JSON files stored in object storage:

Using SQL:

```
CREATE OR REFRESH LIVE TABLE clickstream_raw
COMMENT "The raw wikipedia clickstream dataset, ingested from datasets."
AS SELECT * FROM json.`/databricks-datasets/wikipedia-datasets/data-001/clickstream/raw-uncompressed-json/2015_2_clickstream.json`;
```

Using Python:

```
import dlt
from pyspark.sql.functions import *

json_path = "/databricks-datasets/wikipedia-datasets/data-001/clickstream/raw-uncompressed-json/2015_2_clickstream.json"

@dlt.table(
  comment="The raw wikipedia clickstream dataset, ingested from datasets."
)
```

```
def clickstream_raw():
  return (spark.read.format("json").load(json_path))
```

User can declare new table that queries from other datasets (like above live table). This creates a dependency that Delta Live Tables automatically resolves before executing updates. The following code creates another Live table which refers to the above created table. It also includes examples of monitoring and enforcing data quality with expectations.

Using SQL:

```
CREATE OR REFRESH LIVE TABLE clickstream_prepared(
  CONSTRAINT valid_current_page EXPECT (current_page_title IS NOT NULL)
)
COMMENT "Wikipedia clickstream data cleaned and prepared for analysis."
AS SELECT
  curr_title AS current_page_title,
  CAST(n AS INT) AS click_count,
  prev_title AS previous_page_title
FROM live.clickstream_raw;
```

Using Python:

```
@dlt.table(
  comment="Wikipedia clickstream data cleaned and prepared for analysis."
)
@dlt.expect("valid_current_page_title", "current_page_title IS NOT NULL")
def clickstream_prepared():
  return (
    dlt.read("clickstream_raw")
      .withColumn("click_count", expr("CAST(n AS INT)"))
      .withColumnRenamed("curr_title", "current_page_title")
      .withColumnRenamed("prev_title", "previous_page_title")
      .select("current_page_title", "click_count", "previous_page_title")
  )
```

The above live table refers to earlier created live table(clickstream_raw). It also enforces the data constraint on the column current_page_title.

Live tables are equivalent conceptually to materialized views. The traditional views execute logic each time the view is queried but live tables store the most recent version of query results in data files.

User can declare highly enriched views that power dashboards, BI, and analytics by declaring tables with specific business logic. The following code creates an enriched materialized view from the *clickstream_prepared* table.

Using SQL:

```sql
CREATE OR REFRESH LIVE TABLE top_spark_referers
COMMENT "A table containing the top pages linking to the Apache Spark page."
AS SELECT
  previous_page_title as referrer,
  click_count
FROM live.clickstream_prepared
WHERE current_page_title = 'Apache_Spark'
ORDER BY click_count DESC
LIMIT 10;
```

Using Python:

```python
@dlt.table(
  comment="A table containing the top pages linking to the Apache Spark page."
)
def top_spark_referrers():
  return (
    dlt.read("clickstream_prepared")
      .filter(expr("current_page_title == 'Apache_Spark'"))
      .withColumnRenamed("previous_page_title", "referrer")
      .sort(desc("click_count"))
      .select("referrer", "click_count")
      .limit(10)
  )
```

The above codes can be put in Databrick notebook which can be scheduled to execute from Delta Live Table pipeline.

If user needs to calculate intermediate tables that are not intended for external consumption, user can prevent them from being published to a schema using the TEMPORARY keyword. Temporary tables still store and process data according to Delta Live Tables semantics but should not be accessed outside of the current pipeline.

To declare temporary table:

```sql
CREATE TEMPORARY LIVE TABLE temp_table
AS SELECT ...;
```

Create Delta live pipeline

User can configure Delta Live Tables pipelines and trigger updates using the Databricks workspace UI or automated tooling options such as the API and CLI.

To create the pipeline:
- Click *Workflows* in the Databricks workspace UI sidebar, click the *Delta Live Tables* tab, and click *Create Pipeline*.
- Specify the pipeline name, product edition, pipeline mode and other details. The pipeline mode is continuous or triggered.

Triggered pipelines update once and then shut down the cluster until the next manual or scheduled update. Continuous pipelines keep an always running cluster that ingests new data as it arrives. This property can be changed as requirements evolve.

To avoid unnecessary processing in continuous execution mode, pipelines automatically monitor dependent Delta tables and perform an update only when the contents of those dependent tables have changed.

Triggered pipelines can reduce resource consumption and expense. However, new data won't be processed until the pipeline is triggered. Continuous pipelines require an always-running cluster, which is more expensive but reduces processing latency.

The following table highlights differences between these execution modes:

	Triggered	**Continuous**
When does the update stop?	Automatically once complete.	Runs continuously until manually stopped.
What data is processed?	Data available when the update is started.	All data as it arrives at configured sources.
What data freshness requirements is this best for?	Data updates run every 10 minutes, hourly, or daily.	Data updates desired between every 10 seconds and a few minutes.

- Choose the notebook path that user wants to run as part of this pipeline. This notebook contains the live table datasets definitions. For each dataset, Delta Live Tables compares the current state with the desired state and proceeds to create or update datasets.

- Choose the destination by specifying a Target schema to publish dataset to the Hive metastore or a Catalog and a Target schema to publish the dataset to Unity Catalog.

Storage options

○ Hive Metastore ● Unity Catalog Preview

If user does not specify a target for publishing data, tables created in Delta Live Tables pipelines can only be accessed by other operations within that same pipeline.
- Define the cluster policy where user specifies the autoscaling options.
- Click **Notifications** to configure one or more email addresses to receive notifications for pipeline events. Notifications will be sent when the following occurs:
    - o A pipeline update completes successfully.
    - o Each time a pipeline update fails.
    - o A single data flow fails.

Data access permissions are configured through the cluster used for execution. Make sure that cluster has appropriate permissions configured for data sources and the target storage location.

Once a pipeline is configured, user can trigger a pipeline update to calculate results for each dataset in pipeline.

Pipeline update
Once user creates a pipeline and are ready to run it, user starts an *update*. This is starting the pipeline. To start an update for a pipeline, click the "Start" button in the top panel. The system returns a message confirming that the pipeline is starting.

After successfully starting the pipeline, the Delta Live Table system:
- Starts a cluster using the defined cluster configuration.
- Creates tables that don't exist and ensures that the schema is correct for any existing tables.
- Updates tables with the latest data available.
- Shuts down the cluster when the update is complete.

Pipelines can be run continuously or on a schedule depending on cost and latency requirements.

The tables and views updated. Tables and views are updated based on the update type:

- *Refresh all*: All live tables are updated to reflect the current state of their input data sources. For all streaming tables, new rows are appended to the table.
- *Full refresh all*: All live tables are updated to reflect the current state of their input data sources. For all streaming tables, Delta Live Tables attempts to clear all data from each table and then load all data from the streaming source.

- *Refresh selection*: The behaviour of refresh selection is identical to refresh all but allows us to refresh only selected tables. For selected streaming tables, new rows are appended to the table.
- *Full refresh selection*: The behaviour of full refresh selection is identical to full refresh all but allows to perform a full refresh of only selected tables.

User can use selective refresh with only triggered pipelines.

Schedule a pipeline

User can start a triggered pipeline manually or run the pipeline on a schedule with an Azure Databricks job.

To create a single-task job and a schedule for the job in the Delta Live Tables UI:
- Click Schedule > Add a schedule.
- Enter a name for the job in the Job name field.
- Set the Schedule to Scheduled.
- Specify the period, starting time, and time zone.
- Configure one or more email addresses to receive alerts on pipeline start, success, or failure.
- Click Create.

User can run a Delta Live Tables pipeline as part of a data processing workflow with Apache Airflow, or Azure Data Factory. User can call Delta Live Tables API from an Azure Data Factory Web activity to trigger the pipeline from Azure Data factory.

Data quality

User can use expectations to specify data quality controls on the contents of a dataset. Expectations are optional clauses user adds to Delta Live Tables dataset declarations that apply data quality checks on each record passing through a query.

Maintenance tasks

Delta Live Tables performs maintenance tasks within 24 hours of a table being updated. Maintenance can improve query performance and reduce cost by removing old versions of tables. System performs a full OPTIMIZE operation followed by VACUUM. User can disable OPTIMIZE for a table by setting pipelines.autoOptimize.managed = false in the table properties for the table. Maintenance tasks are performed only if a pipeline update has run in the 24 hours before the maintenance tasks are scheduled.

Development and production modes

Pipeline execution can be optimized by switching between development and production modes. Use the Development or production buttons in the Pipelines UI to switch between Development or production modes. By default, pipelines run in development mode.

When pipeline is run in development mode, the Delta Live Tables system does the following:

- Reuses a cluster to avoid the overhead of restarts. By default, clusters run for two hours when development mode is enabled. To change the value, user can define pipelines.clusterShutdown.delay setting in the configuration of compute settings as shown below. In the figure below, the cluster shutdown has been configured to 60 seconds.

JSON   📋 Copy

```
{
    "configuration": {
        "pipelines.clusterShutdown.delay": "60s"
    }
}
```

- Disables pipeline retries so user can immediately detect and fix errors.

In production mode, the Delta Live Tables system does the following: -
- Restarts the cluster for specific recoverable errors, including memory leaks and stale credentials.
- Retries execution in the event of specific errors, e.g., a failure to start a cluster.
- In **production** mode, the default value for **pipelines.clusterShutdown.delay** is 0 **seconds.** Cluster is always running.

Switching between development and production modes only affects cluster and pipeline execution behaviour. Storage locations and target schemas in the catalog for publishing tables are not affected when switching between modes.

Publish data to Hive metastore

The output data of pipeline can be published to the Hive metastore. To publish datasets to the metastore, enter a schema name in the Target field when user creates a pipeline. User can also add a target database to an existing pipeline.

By default, all tables and views created in Delta Live Tables are local to the pipeline. User must publish tables to a target schema to query or use Delta Live Tables datasets (created outside the pipeline).

If user needs to calculate intermediate tables that are not intended for external consumption, user can prevent them from being published to a schema using the TEMPORARY keyword. Temporary tables still store and process data according to Delta Live Tables semantics, but can't not be accessed outside of the current pipeline. User can define the temporary table in SQL like:

```
CREATE TEMPORARY LIVE TABLE temp_table
AS SELECT ... ;
```

In python, the temporary tables can be defined like: -

```
@dlt.table(
    temporary=True)
def temp_table():
    return ("...")
```

Publish data to Unity Catalog

Unity Catalog can be used with Delta Live Tables pipelines to:
- Define a catalog in Unity Catalog where pipeline will persist data.
- Read data from Unity Catalog tables.

A single pipeline cannot write to both the Hive metastore and Unity Catalog and existing pipelines cannot be upgraded to use Unity Catalog. Existing pipelines that use the Hive metastore cannot be upgraded to use Unity Catalog. To migrate an existing pipeline that writes to Hive metastore, a new pipeline must be created and data need to be re-ingested from the data source.

To create tables in Unity Catalog from a Delta Live Tables pipeline, user must have USE CATALOG privileges on the target catalog, CREATE TABLE and USE SCHEMA privileges in the target schema. User must have CREATE MATERIALIZED VIEW and USE SCHEMA privileges in the target schema if pipeline creates materialized views.

When Delta Live Table is configured to persist data to Unity Catalog, the lifecycle of the table is managed by the Delta Live Tables pipeline.
- When a table is removed from the Delta Live Tables pipeline definition, the corresponding materialized view or streaming table entry is removed from Unity Catalog on the next pipeline execution. The actual data is retained for a period so that it can be recovered if it was deleted by mistake. The data can be recovered by adding the materialized view or streaming table back into the pipeline definition.
- Deleting the Delta Live Tables pipeline results in deletion of all tables defined in that pipeline. Because of this change, the Delta Live Tables UI is updated to prompt user to confirm deletion of a pipeline.

To write tables to Unity Catalog, while creating pipeline, select *Unity Catalog* under *Storage options*, select a catalog in the *Catalog* dropdown menu, and provide a database name in the *Target schema* field.

Ingest data from Unity Catalog

Pipeline configured to use Unity Catalog can read data from Unity Catalog managed and external tables, views, materialized views and streaming tables.

Using SQL:

```sql
CREATE OR REFRESH LIVE TABLE
  table_name
AS SELECT
  *
FROM
  my_catalog.my_schema.table1;
```

Using Python:

```python
@dlt.table
def table_name():
  return spark.table("my_catalog.my_schema.table")
```

Ingest streaming data from Unity Catalog table

In case of streaming changes, the stream can be read.

Using SQL:

```sql
CREATE OR REFRESH STREAMING TABLE
  table_name
AS SELECT
  *
FROM
  STREAM(my_catalog.my_schema.table1);
```

Using Python:

```python
@dlt.table
def table_name():
  return spark.readStream.table("my_catalog.my_schema.table")
```

Ingest data from Hive metastore

A pipeline that uses Unity Catalog can read data from Hive metastore tables using the hive_metastore catalog.

Using SQL:

```sql
CREATE OR REFRESH LIVE TABLE
  table_name
AS SELECT
  *
FROM
  hive_metastore.my_schema.table;
```

Using Python:

```python
@dlt.table
def hivetable():
  return spark.table("hive_metastore.my_schema.table")
```

Ingest data from Auto Loader

The streaming data can be ingested using Auto loader.

SQL:

```sql
CREATE OR REFRESH STREAMING TABLE
  table_name
AS SELECT
  *
FROM
  cloud_files(
    <path-to-uc-external-location>,
    "json"
  )
```

Python:

```python
@dlt.table(table_properties={"quality": "bronze"})
def table_name():
  return (
    spark.readStream.format("cloudFiles")
    .option("cloudFiles.format", "json")
    .load(f"{path_to_uc_external_location}")
  )
```

Share materialized views (live tables)

The tables created by a pipeline can be queried only by the pipeline owner. Other users can be given the ability to query a table by using GRANT statements. Access can be revoked using REVOKE statements.

To grant select on table:

```sql
GRANT SELECT ON TABLE
  my_catalog.my_schema.live_table
TO
  `user@abc.com`
```

To revoke the access:

```
REVOKE SELECT ON TABLE
 my_catalog.my_schema.live_table
FROM
 `user@abc.com`
```

To grant create table privileges, it can be done through:

```
GRANT CREATE TABLE ON SCHEMA
 my_catalog.my_schema
TO
 `user@abc.com`
```

To grant create materialized view privileges, it can be done through:

```
GRANT CREATE MATERIALIZED VIEW ON SCHEMA
 my_catalog.my_schema
TO
 `user@abc.com`
```

Load data with Delta Live Tables

User can load data from any data source supported by Apache Spark on Databricks using Delta Live Tables. User can define datasets (tables and views) in Delta Live Tables against any query that returns a Spark DataFrame.

Load files from cloud object storage

Databricks recommends using Auto Loader with Delta Live Tables for most data ingestion tasks from cloud object storage. Auto Loader and Delta Live Tables are designed to incrementally load ever-growing data as it arrives in cloud storage. The following examples use Auto Loader to create datasets from CSV and JSON files:

Using SQL:

```
CREATE OR REFRESH STREAMING TABLE customers
AS SELECT * FROM cloud_files("/databricks-datasets/retail-org/customers/", "csv")

CREATE OR REFRESH STREAMING TABLE sales_orders_raw
AS SELECT * FROM cloud_files("/databricks-datasets/retail-org/sales_orders/", "json")
```

Using Python:-

```
@dlt.table
def customers():
  return (
    spark.readStream.format("cloudFiles")
      .option("cloudFiles.format", "csv")
      .load("/databricks-datasets/retail-org/customers/")
  )



@dlt.table
def sales_orders_raw():
  return (
    spark.readStream.format("cloudFiles")
      .option("cloudFiles.format", "json")
      .load("/databricks-datasets/retail-org/sales_orders/")
  )
```

Load data from a message bus

User can configure Delta Live Tables pipelines to ingest data from message buses with streaming tables. The following code configures a streaming table to ingest data from Kafka:

```
import dlt
@dlt.table
def kafka_raw():
  return (
    spark.readStream
      .format("kafka")
      .option("kafka.bootstrap.servers", "<server:ip>")
      .option("subscribe", "topic1")
      .option("startingOffsets", "latest")
      .load()
  )
```

User can write subsequent operations in pure SQL to perform streaming transformations on this data as shown below:

```
CREATE OR REFRESH STREAMING TABLE streaming_silver_table
AS SELECT
  *
FROM
  STREAM(LIVE.kafka_raw)
WHERE ...
```

Load data from Postgresql table

The following example declares a materialized view to access the current state of data in a remote Postgresql table.

```
import dlt
@dlt.table
def postgres_raw():
 return (
  spark.read
   .format("postgresql")
   .option("dbtable", table_name)
   .option("host", database_host_url)
   .option("port", 5432)
   .option("database", database_name)
   .option("user", username)
   .option("password", password)
   .load()
 )
```

Load data from JSON table

The following example demonstrates loading JSON to create Delta Live Tables.

Using SQL:
```
CREATE OR REFRESH LIVE TABLE clickstream_raw
AS SELECT * FROM json.`/databricks-datasets/.../2015_2_clickstream.json`
```

Using Python:
```
@dlt.table
def clickstream_raw():
 return (spark.read.format("json").load("/databricks-datasets/... /2015_2_clickstream.json"))
```

For direct file access using SQL with Delta Live Tables, user can use command like shown below. This SQL construct is common to all SQL environments on Databricks.

```
SELECT * FROM format.`path`
```

Manage data quality with Delta Live Tables

Expectations are used to define data quality constraints on the contents of a dataset. Expectations provide guarantee that data arriving in tables meets data quality requirements. Expectations can be applied using Python decorators or SQL constraint clauses.

Delta Live Tables expectations

Expectations are optional clauses that can be added to Delta Live Tables dataset declarations. Expectations apply data quality checks on each record passing through a query.

An expectation consists of three things:
- A description, which acts as a unique identifier and allows to track metrics for the constraint.
- A boolean statement that always returns true or false based on some stated condition.
- An action to take when a record fails the expectation, meaning the boolean returns false.

User can apply three actions on invalid records:
- *warn(default)*: Invalid records are written to the target. Failure is reported as a metric for the dataset.
- *drop*: Invalid records are dropped before data is written to the target. Failure is reported as a metrics for the dataset.
- *fail*: Invalid records prevent the update from succeeding. Manual intervention is required before re-processing.

Data quality metrics such as the number of records can be viewed that violate an expectation by querying the Delta Live Table event log.

- *Retail invalid records*: Use the **expect** operator when user wants to keep records that violate the expectation. Records that violate the expectation are added to the target dataset along with valid records.

  Using Python:
  ```
  @dlt.expect("valid timestamp", "col(“timestamp”) > '2012-01-01'")
  ```

  Using SQL:
  ```
  CONSTRAINT valid_timestamp EXPECT (timestamp > '2012-01-01')
  ```

- *Drop Invalid records*: Use the **expect** or **drop** operator to prevent further processing of invalid records. Records that violate the expectation are dropped from the target dataset.

  Using SQL:
  ```
  CONSTRAINT valid_current_page EXPECT (current_page_id IS NOT NULL and current_page_title IS NOT NULL) ON VIOLATION DROP ROW
  ```

  Using python:
  ```
  @dlt.expect_or_drop("valid_current_page", "current_page_id IS NOT NULL AND current_page_title IS NOT NULL")
  ```

- *Fail on invalid records*:

  When invalid records are unacceptable, use the *expect_or_fail* operator to stop execution immediately when a record fails validation. If the operation is a table update, the system atomically rolls back the transaction.

  Using Python:

  ```
  @dlt.expect_or_fail("valid_count", "count > 0")
  ```

  Using SQL:

  ```
  CONSTRAINT valid_count EXPECT (count > 0) ON VIOLATION FAIL UPDATE
  ```

  When a pipeline fails because of an expectation violation, User must fix the pipeline code to handle the invalid data correctly before re-running the pipeline.

Multiple expectations

User can define expectations with one or more data quality constraints in Python pipelines.

- *expect_all*: Use expect_all to specify multiple data quality constraints when records that fail validation should be included in the target dataset.
- *expect_all_or_drop*:- Use expect_all_or_drop to specify multiple data quality constraints when records that fail validation should be dropped from the target dataset:
- *expect_all_or_fail* : Use expect_all_or_fail to specify multiple data quality constraints when records that fail validation should halt pipeline execution.

  ```
  valid_pages = {"valid_count": "count > 0", "valid_current_page": "current_page_id IS NOT NULL AND current_page_title IS NOT NULL"}
  ```

  ```
  @dlt.table
  @dlt.expect_all(valid_pages)
  def raw_data():
    # Create raw dataset
  ```

  ```
  @dlt.table
  @dlt.expect_all_or_drop(valid_pages)
  def prepared_data():
    # Create cleaned and prepared dataset)
  ```

  In the example above, user is ingesting raw data through raw_data() table where user is ingesting all data even if the condition fails of validation. In the next live table, the table prepared_data is taking only the data which is validated.

Data Transformation

Apache Spark built-in operations, UDFs and custom logic can be used as transformations in Delta Live Tables pipeline. After transformation, user can create new streaming tables, materialized views, and views. Output of transformation are views, materialized views, and streaming tables.

To ensure pipelines are efficient and maintainable, user should choose the best dataset type while implementing pipeline queries.

User should go for view when:

- User have a large or complex query that user wants to break into easier-to-manage queries.
- User wants to validate intermediate results using expectations.
- User wants to reduce storage and compute costs and do not require the materialization of query results. Views are computed on demand. The view is re-computed every time the view is queried.

User should go for materialized view when:
- Materialized views are especially useful in situations where complex queries or aggregations are performed frequently, and the underlying data changes infrequently. By storing the pre-computed results, the database can avoid the need to execute complex queries repeatedly, resulting in faster response times. This precomputation of data allows for faster query response times and improved performance in certain scenarios.
- Materialized view can be consumed by other pipelines, jobs & queries because a materialized view is a database object that stores the results of a query as a physical table.

User should go for streaming table when:
- A query is defined against a data source that is continuously or incrementally growing.
- Query results should be computed incrementally.
- High throughput and low latency are desired for the pipeline.

User can combine streaming tables and materialized views in a single pipeline. In streaming tables, where new rows are always inserted into the source table rather than modified.

A common streaming pattern includes ingesting source data to create the initial datasets in a pipeline. These initial datasets are commonly called *bronze* tables and often perform simple transformations. By contrast, the final tables in a pipeline, commonly referred to as *gold* tables, often require complicated aggregations. These transformations are better suited for materialized views.

The following examples illustrates streaming Bronze, streaming Silver & materialized view gold table.

```python
@dlt.table
def streaming_bronze():
 return (
   # Since this is a streaming source, this table is incremental.
   spark.readStream.format("cloudFiles")
     .option("cloudFiles.format", "json")
     .load("abfss://path_to_raw_data")
 )

@dlt.table
def streaming_silver():
  # Since user read the bronze table as a stream, this silver table is also
  # updated incrementally.
  return dlt.read_stream("streaming_bronze").where(...)

@dlt.table
def live_gold():
  # This table will be recomputed completely by reading the whole silver table when it is updated.
  Return dlt.read("streaming_silver").groupBy("user_id").count()
```

As can be seen from the above example, the streaming_bronze live table takes data from stream source. The silver live table streaming_silver takes data from streaming_bronze live table. The gold live table live_gold is not streaming. It is updated based on data of whole silver table. The live_gold table is materialized view. The Gold table inherently create updates rather than append so they are not supported as streaming tables.

The same can be implemented using SQL as shown below:

```sql
CREATE OR REFRESH STREAMING TABLE streaming_bronze
AS SELECT * FROM cloud_files(
  "abfss://path_to_raw_data", "json"
)

CREATE OR REFRESH STREAMING TABLE streaming_silver
AS SELECT * FROM STREAM(LIVE.streaming_bronze) WHERE...

CREATE OR REFRESH LIVE TABLE live_gold
AS SELECT count(*) FROM LIVE.streaming_silver GROUP BY user_id
```

The streaming table can be joined with any static dimension table to get more information as shown below.

Using SQL:

```
CREATE OR REFRESH STREAMING TABLE customer_sales
AS SELECT * FROM STREAM(LIVE.sales)
  INNER JOIN LEFT LIVE.customers USING (customer_id)
```

Using Python:

```
@dlt.table
def customer_sales():
  return dlt.read_stream("sales").join(read("customers"), ["customer_id"], "left")
```

User can use streaming tables to incrementally calculate simple distributive aggregates like count, min, max, or sum, and algebraic aggregates like average or standard deviation.

Change Data Capture

User can use change data capture (CDC) in Delta Live Tables to incrementally update tables based on changes in source data. CDC is supported in the Delta Live Tables. Delta Live Tables supports updating tables with slowly changing dimensions (SCD) type 1 and type 2.

- SCD type 1 is used to update records directly. History is not retained for records that are updated.
- SCD type 2 is used to retain a history of records, either on all updates or on updates to a specified set of columns.

Change data capture will be discussed in detail in later chapters.

Pipeline settings

Delta Live Tables provides a user interface for configuring and editing pipeline settings. The UI also provides an option to display and edit settings in JSON. Some advanced options are only available using the JSON configuration. The following are some of the pipeline settings that can be configured by user.

Product Edition

The following product editions are available.
- *Core*: - Select core to run streaming ingest workloads. Select the **Core** edition if pipeline doesn't require advanced features such as change data capture (CDC) or Delta Live Tables expectations.
- *Pro*: - Select Pro to run streaming ingest and change data capture (CDC) workloads. The **Pro** product edition supports all the **Core** features, plus support for workloads that require updating tables based on changes in source data.

- *Advanced*: - Select Advanced to run streaming ingest workloads, change data capture (CDC) workloads, and workloads that require expectations. The **Advanced** product edition supports the features of the **Core** and **Pro** editions and supports enforcement of data quality constraints with Delta Live Table expectations.

Pipeline mode

User can choose to update pipeline continuously or with manual triggers. If the pipeline uses the *triggered* execution mode, the system stops processing after successfully refreshing all tables or selected tables in the pipeline.

If the pipeline uses *continuous* execution, Delta Live Tables processes new data as it arrives in data sources to keep tables throughout the pipeline fresh.

Both materialized views and streaming tables can be updated in either execution mode.

Storage Location

User must specify storage location for a pipeline that publishes to the Hive metastore. The primary motivation for specifying a location is to control the object storage location for data written by pipeline.

All tables, data, checkpoints, and metadata for Delta Live Tables pipelines are fully managed by Delta Live Tables. Most interaction with Delta Live Tables datasets happens through tables registered to the Hive metastore or Unity Catalog.

Target schema

While optional, User should specify a target to publish tables created by pipeline. Publishing a pipeline to a target makes datasets available for querying elsewhere in Databricks environment. User can define target schema in Hive metastore or unity catalog.

Autoscaling

Use Enhanced Autoscaling to optimize the cluster utilization of pipelines. Enhanced Autoscaling adds additional resources only if the system determines those resources will increase pipeline processing speed. Resources are freed when they are no longer needed, and clusters are shut down as soon as all pipeline updates are complete.

While configuring Enhanced Autoscaling for production pipelines:

- Leave the Min workers setting at the default.
- Set the Max workers setting to a value based on budget and pipeline priority.

Delay Compute Shutdown

Delta Live Tables cluster automatically shuts down when not in use. To control cluster shutdown behaviour, user can use `pipelines.clusterShutdown.delay` setting in the pipeline configuration. The following example sets the `pipelines.clusterShutdown.delay` value to 60 seconds.

```
{
  "configuration": {
    "pipelines.clusterShutdown.delay": "60s"
  }
}
```

When production mode is enabled, the default value for pipelines.clusterShutdown.delay is 0 seconds. When development mode is enabled, the default value is 2 hours.

Monitor Pipelines

User can use built-in features in Delta Live Tables for monitoring and observability for pipelines, including data lineage, update history, and data quality reporting. Most monitoring data can be reviewed manually through the pipeline details UI. Some information can be found by querying the event log metadata.

The pipeline graph displays as soon as an update to a pipeline has successfully started. Dependencies between datasets in pipeline are represented by arrows. Details displayed include the pipeline ID, source libraries, compute cost, product edition, Databricks Runtime version, and the channel configured for the pipeline. The *Run as* user is the pipeline owner.

To receive real-time notifications for pipeline events like successful completion of a pipeline update or failure of a pipeline update, user can add email notifications for pipeline events.

The Delta Live Tables event log contains all information related to a pipeline, including audit logs, data quality checks, pipeline progress, and data lineage. User can use the event log to track, understand, and monitor the state of data pipelines.

User can view event log entries in the Delta Live Tables user interface, the Delta Live Tables API, or by directly querying the event log.

Querying the event log

The location of the event log and the interface to query the event log depend on whether pipeline is configured to use the Hive metastore or Unity Catalog.

- *Hive Metastore*: If pipeline publishes tables to the Hive metastore, the event log is stored in */system/events* under the storage location. If user has configured pipeline storage setting as */Users/username/data*, the event log is stored in the */Users/username/data/system/events* path in DBFS.

  If user has not configured the storage setting, the default event log location is */pipelines/<pipeline-id>/system/events* in DBFS e.g., if the ID of pipeline is `91de5e48-35ed-11ec-1d4d-0242ac130003`, the storage location is: `/pipelines/91de5e48-35ed-11ec-1d4d-0242ac130003/system/events`.

40

User can create a view to simplify querying the event log like shown below:

```
CREATE OR REPLACE TEMP VIEW event_log_raw AS SELECT * FROM delta.`<event-log-path>`
```

Specify event log location in event-log-path. This creates event_log_raw temporary view. From the view, user can query and get details about various events.

- *Unity Catalog*: If pipeline publishes tables to Unity Catalog, user must use the event_log table valued function (TVF) to fetch the event log for the pipeline. User can retrieve the event log for a pipeline by passing the pipeline ID or a table name to the TVF. To retrieve the event log records for the pipeline with ID, use the command like shown below. Pipeline id should be provided as part of event_log parameter.

```
SELECT * FROM event_log("04c78631-3dd7-
4856-b2a6-7d84e9b2638b")
```

If user doesn't know the pipeline id but wants to get the event_log of the pipeline that created or owns table `my_catalog.my_schema.table1`, then use the below command where table name is provided as input.

```
SELECT * FROM event_log(TABLE(my_catalog.my_schema.table1))
```

To call event_log function, user must use shared cluster or a SQL warehouse. So, queries should be called as shown above from the notebook attached to a shared cluster or use the

SQL editor connected to a SQL warehouse. The event_log TVF can be called only by the pipeline owner. So, to simplify querying events for a pipeline, the owner of the pipeline can create a view over the **event_log** function.

```
CREATE VIEW event_log_raw AS SELECT * FROM event_log("<pipeline-ID>")
```

Query lineage information

Events containing information about lineage have the event type flow_definition. The details:flow_definition object contains the output_dataset and input_datasets defining each relationship in the graph. The below query provides the lineage information.

```
SELECT
 details:flow_definition.output_dataset as output_dataset,
 details:flow_definition.input_datasets as input_dataset
FROM
 event_log_raw
WHERE
 event_type = 'flow_definition'
```

event_log_raw has been created in the previous section.

Query data quality

If user defines expectations on datasets in pipeline, the data quality metrics are stored in the `details:flow_progress.data_quality.expectations` object. Events containing information about data quality have the event type `flow_progress`.

Monitor data backlog

Delta Live Tables tracks how much data is present in the backlog in the `details:flow_progress.metrics.backlog_bytes` object. Events containing backlog metrics have the event type `flow_progress`. User can retrieve the backlog data through the below query.

```
SELECT
  timestamp,
  Double(details :flow_progress.metrics.backlog_bytes) as backlog
FROM
  event_log_raw
WHERE
  event_type ='flow_progress'
```

Monitor Enhanced Autoscaling events

The event log captures cluster resizes when Enhanced Autoscaling is enabled in pipeline. Events containing information about Enhanced Autoscaling have the event type `autoscale`. The cluster resizing request information is stored in the `details:autoscale` object .

Monitor compute resource utilization

Cluster_resources event provides metrics on the number of task slots in the cluster, how much those task slots are utilized, and how many tasks are waiting to be scheduled.

When Enhanced Autoscaling is enabled, cluster_resources events also contain metrics for the autoscaling algorithm, including latest_requested_num_executors and optimal_num_executors.

The following example queries the task queue size history

```
SELECT
  timestamp,
  Double(details :cluster_resources.avg_num_queued_tasks) as queue_size
FROM
  event_log_raw
WHERE
  event_type = 'cluster_resources'
```

User can query many metrics like:

- avg_task_slot_utilization
- num_executors
- latest_requested_num_executors
- optimal_num_executors
- state

Query user actions in the event log

User can use the event log to audit events. Events containing information about user actions have the event type user_action. Information about the action is stored in the user_action object in the details field.

SELECT timestamp, details:user_action:action, details:user_action:user_name FROM event_log_raw WHERE event_type = 'user_action'

	timestamp	action	user_name
1	2021-05-20T19:36:03.517+0000	START	user@abc.com
2	2021-05-20T19:35:59.913+0000	CREATE	user@abc.com
3	2021-05-27T00:35:51.971+0000	START	user@abc.com

User can view runtime information for a pipeline update, for example, the Databricks Runtime version for the update.

SELECT details:create_update:runtime_version:dbr_version FROM event_log_raw WHERE event_type = 'create_update'

Structured Streaming

User can use Databricks for near real-time data ingestion, processing, machine learning, and AI for streaming data. Databricks offers numerous optimizations for streaming and incremental processing. For most streaming or incremental data processing or ETL tasks, Databricks recommends Delta Live Tables.

Most incremental and streaming workloads on Databricks are powered by Structured Streaming, including Delta Live Tables and Auto Loader.

Apache Spark Structured Streaming is a near-real time processing engine that offers end-to-end fault tolerance with exactly-once processing guarantees. The Structured Streaming engine performs the computation incrementally and continuously updates the result as streaming data arrives.

Databricks recommends using Auto Loader to ingest supported file types from cloud object storage into Delta Lake. For ETL pipelines, Databricks recommends using Delta Live Tables (which uses Delta tables and Structured Streaming).

In addition to Delta Lake and Auto Loader, Structured Streaming can connect to messaging services such as Apache Kafka.

User can use Structured Streaming for near real-time and incremental processing workloads. Databricks recommends using Delta Live Tables for Structured Streaming workloads.

Read from a data stream.

User can use Structured Streaming to incrementally ingest data from supported data sources. Structured Streaming workloads supports the following data sources:

- Data files in cloud object storage
- Message buses and queues
- Delta Lake

Databricks recommends using Auto Loader for streaming ingestion from cloud object storage.

Auto Loader to read streaming data

The following example demonstrates loading JSON data (present in cloud object storage) with Auto Loader, which uses **cloudFiles** to denote format and options. The **schemaLocation** option enables schema inference and evolution.

```
raw_df = (spark.readStream
  .format("cloudFiles")
  .option("cloudFiles.format", "json")
  .option("cloudFiles.schemaLocation", "<path-to-schema-location>")
  .load(file_path))
```

file_path is the path of JSON file or folder containing JSON files.

Configuring a streaming read (As shown above) does not actually load data. User must trigger an action on the data before the stream begins e.g. calling display() on a streaming DataFrame starts a streaming job.

Structured Streaming supports most transformations that are available in Databricks and Spark SQL.

Write to a data Sink

A data sink is the target of a streaming write operation. Common sinks used in Azure Databricks streaming workloads include the following:

- Delta Lake
- Message buses and queues
- Key-value databases

Most data sinks provide several options to control how data is written to the target system. During writer configuration, the main options user might need to set fall into the following categories:

- Output mode (append by default).
- A checkpoint location (required for each writer).
- Trigger intervals
- Options that specify the data sink or format (for example, file type, delimiters, and schema).
- Options that configure access to target systems (for example, port settings and credentials).

Incremental batch write

The below code does the incremental batch write for stream. User needs to specify the target location for write and checkpoint location.

```
transformed_df.writeStream
    .trigger(availableNow=True)
    .option("checkpointLocation", checkpoint_path)
    .option("path", target_path)
    .start()
```

The *availableNow* setting for the trigger instructs Structured Streaming to process all previously unprocessed records from the source dataset.

Read data from Delta Lake

To read the data from stream, it can be done through the code:

```
spark.readStream.table("<table-name1>")
```

Write to Delta Lake

To write to a delta table, it can be done through the code:

```
df.writeStream
  .format("delta")
  .outputMode("append")
  .option("checkpointLocation", "/tmp/delta/events/_checkpoints/")
  .toTable("events")
```

The above example will write the streaming data to events table. User must have proper permissions configured to read source tables and write to target tables and the specified checkpoint location.

Read data from Kafka, transform, and write to Kafka

Apache Kafka and other messaging buses provide some of the lowest latency available for large datasets. User can use Databricks to apply transformations to data ingested from Kafka and then write data back to Kafka.

The following is an example for a streaming read from Kafka:

```
df = (spark.readStream
  .format("kafka")
  .option("kafka.bootstrap.servers", "<server:ip>")
  .option("subscribe", "<topic>")
  .option("startingOffsets", "latest")
  .load())
```

To write data to kafka:

```
df.writeStream
  .format("kafka")
  .option("kafka.bootstrap.servers", "<server:ip>")
  .option("topic", "<topic>")
  .option("checkpointLocation", "<checkpoint-path>")
  .start()
```

Using Unity Catalog with Structured Streaming

Use Structured Streaming with Unity Catalog to manage data governance for incremental and streaming workloads on Databricks. The Unity Catalog data governance model allows to stream data from managed and external tables in Unity Catalog. User can write data to external tables using either table names or file paths. Use table name to interact with managed tables on Unity Catalog.

Streaming with Delta lake

Delta Lake is deeply integrated with Spark Structured Streaming through readStream and writeStream. Delta Lake has the following benefits.

- Coalescing small files produced by low latency ingest
- Maintaining "exactly-once" processing with more than one stream (or concurrent batch jobs)
- Efficiently discovering which files are new when using files as the source for a stream

When user loads a Delta table as a stream source and use it in a streaming query, the query processes all of the data present in the table as well as any new data that arrives after the stream is started.

spark.readStream.format("delta").load("Delta_file_path")

If the schema for a Delta table changes after a streaming read begins against the table, the query fails.

Limit input rate

The following options are available to control micro-batches:

- maxFilesPerTrigger: How many new files to be considered in every micro-batch. The default is 1000.
- maxBytesPerTrigger: How much data gets processed in each micro-batch.

If user uses maxBytesPerTrigger in conjunction with maxFilesPerTrigger, the micro-batch processes data until either the maxFilesPerTrigger or maxBytesPerTrigger limit is reached.

Structured Streaming does not handle input that is not an append and throws an exception if any modifications occur on the table being used as a source. There are two main strategies for dealing with changes:

- User can delete the output and checkpoint and restart the stream from the beginning.
- User can set either of these two options:
  - ignoreDeletes: ignore transactions that delete data at partition boundaries (the WHERE is on a partition column).

    spark.readStream.format("delta").option("ignoreDeletes", "true").load("Delta_file_path")

  - skipChangeCommits: ignore transactions that delete or modify existing records. skipChangeCommits includes ignoreDeletes.

Specify Initial position:

User can specify the starting point of the Delta Lake streaming source without processing the entire table. The options to do this are:

- StartingVersion: The Delta Lake version to start from. All table changes starting from this version (inclusive) will be read by the streaming source. The commit versions can be obtained from the version column of the DESCRIBE HISTORY command output. In the example below, the changes are read from version 5 for user_events table.

```
spark.readStream.format("delta").option("startingVersion", "5").load("/tmp/delta/user_events")
```

- StartingTimestamp: The timestamp to start from. All table changes committed at or after the timestamp (inclusive) will be read by the streaming source. In the example below, changes are read since 2018-10-18, use:

```
spark.readStream.format("delta").option("startingTimestamp", "2018-10-
18").load("/tmp/delta/user_events")
```

Delta table as a sink

User can write data into a Delta table using Structured Streaming. The transaction log enables Delta Lake to guarantee exactly once processing, even when there are other streams or batch queries running concurrently against the table.

By default, streams run in append mode, which adds new records to the table.

```
events.writeStream.format("delta")
.outputMode("append")
.option("checkpointLocation", "/tmp/delta/_checkpoints/")
.start("/delta/events")
```

To save the data in table, use the code like:

```
events.writeStream
.format("delta")
.outputMode("append")
.option("checkpointLocation", "/tmp/delta/events/_checkpoints/")
.toTable("events")
```

User can also use Structured Streaming to replace the entire table with every batch. User has to use complete mode for outputmode like:

```
events.writeStream
.format("delta")
.outputMode("complete")
.option("checkpointLocation", "/tmp/delta/events/_checkpoints/")
.toTable("events")
```

Performing stream-static joins

User can rely on the transactional guarantees and versioning protocol of Delta Lake to perform *stream-static* joins. A stream-static join joins the latest valid version of a Delta table (the static data) to a data stream using a stateless join. As can be seen below, inner join is done between streaming data & static dataframe.

```
streamingDF = spark.readStream.table("orders")
staticDF = spark.read.table("customers")

query = (streamingDF
  .join(staticDF, streamingDF.customer_id==staticDF.id, "inner")
  .writeStream
  .option("checkpointLocation", checkpoint_path)
  .table("orders_with_customer_info")
)
```

Processing results from streaming queries using foreachBatch

User can use a combination of **merge** and **foreachBatch** to write complex upserts from a streaming query into a Delta table.

```
from delta.tables import *
deltaTable = DeltaTable.forPath(spark, "/data/aggregates")

# Function to upsert microBatchOutputDF into Delta table using merge
def upsertToDelta(microBatchOutputDF, batchId):
  (deltaTable.alias("t").merge(
    microBatchOutputDF.alias("s"),
    "s.key = t.key")
  .whenMatchedUpdateAll()
  .whenNotMatchedInsertAll()
  .execute()
  )
```

```
# Write the output of a streaming aggregation query into Delta table by call above function
```

```
(streamingAggregatesDF.writeStream
 .format("delta")
 .foreachBatch(upsertToDelta)
 .outputMode("update")
 .start()
)
```

This way the micro batch output of streaming can be processed for upsert or any other transformation.

Write to Azure Synapse Analytics

User can write the output of a streaming query to Azure Synapse Analytics using foreachBatch function of writeStream. It takes each batch of data and write to Azure synapse analytics. In the example below, writeToSQLWarehouse function is used to write the batch of data to Azure synapse analytics. The function is called during stream write.

```
from pyspark.sql.functions import *
from pyspark.sql import *
```

```
def writeToSQLWarehouse(df, epochId):
 df.write \
   .format("com.databricks.spark.sqldw") \
   .mode('overwrite') \
   .option("url", "jdbc:sqlserver://<the-rest-of-the-connection-string>") \
   .option("forward_spark_azure_storage_credentials", "true") \
   .option("dbtable", "my_table_in_dw_copy") \
   .option("tempdir", "wasbs://<your-container-name>@<your-storage-account-
name>.blob.core.windows.net/<your-directory-name>") \
   .save()
```

```
# Write the output of a streaming aggregation query into synapse analytics
(streamingAggregatesDF.writeStream
 .format("delta")
 .foreachBatch(writeToSQLWarehouse)
 .outputMode("update")
 .start()
)
```

Write to any location using foreachBatch

streamingDF.writeStream.foreachBatch function allows to specify a function that is executed on the output data of every micro-batch of the streaming query. It takes two parameters: a

DataFrame or Dataset that has the output data of a micro-batch and the unique ID of the micro-batch.

If user wants to write the output of a streaming query to multiple locations, then user can simply write the output DataFrame/Dataset multiple times in the foreachBatch function, but each attempt to write can cause the output data to be recomputed (including possible re-reading of the input data). To avoid recomputation, user should cache the output DataFrame/Dataset, write it to multiple locations, and then uncache it. So, in the foreachbatch function, user should cache this dataframe, do the operation and then uncache it.

In the code below, the microbatch dataframe is cached and then this dataframe is written to both places and then it is the uncached.

```
batchDF.persist()
batchDF.write.format(...).save(...) // location 1
batchDF.write.format(...).save(...) // location 2
batchDF.unpersist()
```

Write to any location using foreach()

If user can't use foreachBatch function due to Databricks Runtime lower than 4.2 or corresponding batch data writer does not exist then user can use foreach().

```
def processRow(row):
  // Write row to storage


query = streamingDF.writeStream.foreach(processRow).start()
```

Asynchronous progress tracking

Asynchronous progress tracking allows Structured Streaming pipelines to checkpoint progress asynchronously and in parallel to the actual data processing within a micro-batch.

Asynchronous progress tracking enables Structured Streaming pipelines to checkpoint progress without being impacted by the offset management operations.

```
stream = spark.readStream
  .format("kafka")
  .option("kafka.bootstrap.servers", "host1:port1,host2:port2")
  .option("subscribe", "in")
  .load()


stream.writeStream
  .format("kafka")
  .option("topic", "out")
```

```
.option("checkpointLocation", "/tmp/checkpoint")
.option("asyncProgressTrackingEnabled", "true")
.start()
```

In the example above, user is reading stream from kafka data sources and write the data to a topic. asyncProgressTrackingEnabled is set to true which enables the asynchronous progress tracking.

Apache Spark

Apache Spark is the technology which powers compute clusters and SQL warehouses of Databricks. Databricks provides an efficient and simple platform for running Apache Spark workloads.

When user deploys a compute cluster or SQL warehouse on Databricks, Apache Spark is configured and deployed to virtual machines. Databricks configure or initialize a Spark context or Spark session.

Databricks SQL uses Apache Spark under the hood, but end users use standard SQL syntax to create and query database objects.

PySpark DataFrames

A DataFrame is a two-dimensional labelled data structure with columns of potentially different types. Apache Spark DataFrames provide a rich set of functions (select columns, filter, join, aggregate) that allow user to solve common data analysis problems efficiently.

Spark DataFrames and Spark SQL use a unified planning and optimization engine and hence user will get identical performance across all supported languages on Databricks (Python, SQL, Scala, and R).

Create a DataFrame

Most Apache Spark queries return a DataFrame. This includes reading from a table, loading data from files, and operations that transform data.

User can create a Spark DataFrame from a list or a panda DataFrame, such as in the following example:

To create spark dataframe from panda dataframe(pdf):

```
df1 = spark.createDataFrame(pdf)
```

To create spark DataFrame from list:

```
import pandas as pd
data = [[1, "Elia"], [2, "Teo"], [3, "Fang"]]
df2 = spark.createDataFrame(data, schema="id LONG, name STRING")
```

Create a DataFrame from catalog table

User can load catalog tables to DataFrames through the below code:

```
df= spark.read.table("<catalog-name>.<schema-name>.<table-name>")
```

Load data from csv file

User can load csv file to a dataframe using the below syntax:

```
df = (spark.read
  .format("csv")
  .option("header", "true")
  .option("inferSchema", "true")
  .load("csv_file_path")
)
```

Combine DataFrames with join and union

Dataframes use standard SQL semantics for join operations. A join returns the combined results of two dataframes based on the provided matching conditions and join type. The following example is an inner join between dataframes df1 & df2 based on "id" column. The output dataframe is joined_df.

```
joined_df = df1.join(df2, how="inner", on="id")
```

User can add the combine two dataframes using the union operation, as in the following example:

```
unioned_df = df1.union(df2)
```

Filter rows in a DataFrame

User can filter rows in a DataFrame using *filter* or *where*. There is no difference in performance or syntax. To get records of dataframe df having id value more than 1, it can be done through the following code:

```
filtered_df = df.filter("id > 1")
filtered_df = df.where("id > 1")
```

Select columns from a DataFrame

User can select columns by passing one or more column names to **select function.**

```
select_df = df.select("id", "name")
```

View the DataFrame

To view the data in a tabular format, user can use the Databricks *display* command.

```
display(df)
```

Print the data schema

User can print the schema using the printSchema() method.

```
df.printSchema()
```

Save a DataFrame to a table

Databricks uses Delta Lake for all tables by default. User can save the contents of a DataFrame to a table using the following syntax:

```
df.write.saveAsTable("<table-name>")
```

Run SQL queries in PySpark

Spark Dataframes provide several options to combine SQL with Python. The selectExpr() method allows to specify each column as a SQL query, such as in the following example:

```
display(df.selectExpr("id", "upper(name) as big_name"))
```

User can import the *expr* function from `pyspark.sql.functions` to use SQL syntax anywhere a column would be specified, as in the following example:

```
from pyspark.sql.functions import expr
display(df.select("id", expr("lower(name) as little_name")))
```

User can use spark.sql() to run SQL queries in the Python kernel, as in the following example:

```
query_df = spark.sql("SELECT * FROM <table-name>")
```

Because logic is executed in the Python kernel and all SQL queries are passed as strings, user can use Python formatting to parameterize SQL queries, as in the following example. query_df contains the result of sql query as dataframe.

```
table_name = "my_table"
query_df = spark.sql(f"SELECT * FROM {table_name}")
```

Clusters

A Databricks cluster is a set of computation resources and configurations on which data engineering, data science, and data analytics workloads are run.

These workloads are run as a set of commands in a notebook or as an automated job. Clusters are of two type, *all-purpose clusters,* and *job clusters.* All-purpose cluster is used to analyse data collaboratively using interactive notebooks. Job cluster is used to run automated jobs.

- All-purpose cluster can be created using the UI, CLI, or REST API. User can manually terminate and restart an all-purpose cluster. Multiple users can share such clusters to do collaborative interactive analysis.
- The Databricks job scheduler creates a job cluster when user run a job and terminates the cluster when the job is complete. User cannot restart a job cluster.

To create a cluster using the user interface:
- Click Compute in the sidebar and then Create compute on the Compute page.
- Choose the compute option and create the cluster.

Cluster policy

Cluster policies are a set of rules used to limit the configuration options available to users when they create a cluster. Cluster policies have access control list that regulate which specific users and groups have access to certain policies. While creating cluster, user must specify the cluster policy. By default, all users have access to the Personal Compute policy, allowing them to create single-machine compute resources.

When creating a cluster, users can only select policies for which they have been granted permission. To create cluster policy:

- Click Compute in the sidebar
- Click the **Cluster Policies** tab and create policy.

Cluster access mode

Cluster access mode is a security feature that determines who can use a cluster and what data they can access via the cluster. When user create any cluster in Azure Databricks, user must select an access mode. The access modes are:

- Single user: It is always visible to User. It supports Unity catalog. Supported languages are Python, SQL, Scala, R. Cluster can be assigned to and used by a single user only. Dynamic views are not supported. Credential passthrough is not supported.
- Shared: - It is always (Premium plan required) visible to users. It supports Unity catalog. Supported languages are Python (on Databricks Runtime 11.1 and above), SQL. Cluster can be used by multiple users with data isolation among users.
- No isolation shared: Multiple users can use the same cluster. Users share credentials set at the cluster level. No data access controls are enforced.

Cluster Node Type

A cluster consists of one driver node and zero or more worker nodes. By default, the driver node uses the same instance type as the worker node, but user can choose separate instance types for the driver and worker nodes. Different families of instance types fit different use cases, such as memory-intensive or compute-intensive workloads. Use GPU-enabled clusters for computationally challenging tasks that demand high performance, like those associated with deep learning.

Driver node

The driver node maintains state information of all notebooks attached to the cluster. The driver node also maintains the SparkContext, interprets all the commands user run from a notebook or a library on the cluster, and runs the Apache Spark master that coordinates with the Spark executors.

The default node type of the driver is the same as the worker node type. User can choose a larger driver node type with more memory if user is planning to **collect** a lot of data from Spark workers and analyse them in the notebook.

The command to collect the data for dataframe df:
df.collect()

Worker node

Azure Databricks worker nodes run the Spark executors. When workload is distributed with Spark, all the distributed processing happens on worker nodes. Databricks runs one executor per worker node. The terms executor and worker are used interchangeably in the context of the Databricks architecture.

To run a Spark job, user needs at least one worker node. If a cluster has zero workers, user can run non-spark commands on the driver node, but Spark commands will fail.

Spot instances

To save cost, user can choose to use spot instances by checking the Spot instances checkbox.

Worker Type ❓   **Workers**

| Standard_DS3_v2 | 14.0 GB Memory, 4 Cores, 0.75 DBU | ∨ | 8 | ☑ Spot instance(s) ❓ |

The first instance will always be on-demand (the driver node is always on-demand) and subsequent instances will be spot instances. If spot instances are evicted due to unavailability, on-demand instances are deployed to replace evicted instances.

Cluster size and autoscaling

When user creates an Azure Databricks cluster, user can either provide a fixed number of workers for the cluster or provide a minimum and maximum number of workers for the cluster.

When user provides a fixed size cluster, Databricks ensures that cluster has the specified number of workers. When user provides a range for the number of workers, Databricks chooses the appropriate number of workers required to run job. This is referred to as autoscaling.

Autoscaling makes it easier to achieve high cluster utilization, because user doesn't need to provision the cluster to match a workload. Autoscaling thus offers two advantages:

- Workloads can run faster compared to a constant-sized under-provisioned cluster.
- Autoscaling clusters can reduce overall costs compared to a statically sized cluster.

On the cluster creation and edit page, select the Enable autoscaling checkbox in the Autopilot Options box:

For the Job cluster, On the cluster creation and edit page, select the Enable autoscaling checkbox in the Autopilot Options box:

Autopilot Options
☑ Enable autoscaling ❓

After enabling autoscaling, configure Min & max workers.

Autoscaling local storage

Databricks automatically enables autoscaling local storage on all Databricks clusters. With autoscaling local storage, Databricks monitors the amount of free disk space available on cluster's Spark workers. If a worker begins to run too low on disk, Databricks automatically attaches a new managed disk to the worker before it runs out of disk space. The managed disks attached to a virtual machine are detached only when the virtual machine is returned to cloud provider. Managed disks are never detached from a virtual machine as long as they are part of a running cluster.

Cluster tags

Cluster tags allow to easily monitor the cost of cloud resources used by various groups in organization. User can specify tags as key-value pairs when user creates a cluster.

Spark configuration

User can provide custom Spark configuration properties in a cluster configuration. On the cluster configuration page, click the *Advanced Options* toggle and Click the *Spark* tab. In *Spark config*, enter the configuration properties as one key-value pair per line.

Spark	Tags	Logging	Init Scripts	JDBC/ODBC	Permissions

Spark Config ❔

```
Enter your Spark configuration options here. Provide only one key-value pair per line.
Example:
spark.speculation true
spark.kryo.registrator my.package.MyRegistrator
```

To reference a secret in the Spark configuration through databrick notebook, use the following syntax:

spark.conf.get("spark.<property-name>")

Using SQL, user can get the value using below command:

SELECT ${spark.<property-name>}

Cluster log delivery

When user creates a cluster, user can specify a location to deliver the logs for the Spark driver node, worker nodes, and events. Logs are delivered every five minutes to the chosen destination. Databricks guarantees to deliver all logs generated up until the cluster was terminated.

The destination of the logs depends on the cluster ID. If the specified destination is dbfs:/cluster-log-delivery, cluster logs for id "clustered" are delivered to:

dbfs:/cluster-log-delivery/clustered

To configure the log delivery location:

- On the cluster configuration page, click the **Advanced Options** toggle.
- Click the **Logging** tab.

- Select a destination type.
- Enter the cluster log path.

Personal Compute resource

Personal Compute is an Azure Databricks-managed default cluster policy available on all Databricks workspaces. The policy allows users to easily create single-machine compute resources for their individual use so they can start running workloads immediately, minimizing compute management overhead. Personal compute resources are all-purpose clusters with the following properties:

- Personal Compute resources are single-node clusters. The cluster is having no worker and with spark running in local mode.
- Auto-termination is set at 72 hours.
- Both standard instances and GPU-enabled instances are available

If user doesn't see the Personal Compute policy as an option when user creates a cluster, then user have not been given access to the policy. User should contact administrator to request access to the Personal Compute policy.

To create personal compute cluster, click on *Create Personal Compute.* This will open the cluster configuration dialog with the Personal Compute policy chosen. Click Create Cluster. This will create Personal compute cluster.

User can set auto termination for a cluster. During cluster creation, user can specify an inactivity period in minutes after which user want the cluster to terminate. If the difference between the current time and the last command run on the cluster is more than the inactivity period specified, Databricks automatically terminates that cluster. User can configure automatic termination in the create cluster UI. Ensure that the box is checked and enter the number of minutes in the Terminate after ___ of minutes of inactivity setting.

60

Pools

Databricks pools are a set of idle, ready-to-use instances. When cluster nodes are created using the idle instances, cluster start, and auto-scaling times are reduced. If the pool has no idle instances, the pool expands by allocating a new instance from the instance provider to accommodate the cluster's request. This can lead to increase in time for instance allocation as new instance will be created and allocated. In case of idle instance in pool, since it is already available then allocation is quick, and performance is not impacted. When a cluster releases an instance, it returns to the pool and is free for another cluster to use. Only clusters attached to a pool can use that pool's idle instances.

Creating a pool reduces cluster start and scale-up times by maintaining a set of available, ready-to-use instances. Databricks recommends taking advantage of pools to improve processing time while minimizing cost.

User can specify a different pool for the driver node and worker nodes or use the same pool for both. Azure Databricks does not charge DBUs while instances are idle in the pool. Cloud instance provider billing does apply as idle instance is created by the cloud provider.

If driver node and worker nodes have different requirements, create a different pool for each. User can minimize instance acquisition time by creating a pool for each instance type e.g., if most data engineering clusters use instance type A, data science clusters use instance type B, and analytics clusters use instance type C, create a pool with each instance type.

Pools should be used for job with strict execution times requirements. When cost saving takes priority over reliability then use Pools with spot instances.

Configure pools to control cost:

User can use the following configuration options to help control the cost of pools:

- Set the Min Idle instances to 0 to avoid paying for running instances that aren't doing work. The trade-off is a possible increase in time when a cluster needs to acquire a new instance.
- Set the Idle Instance Auto Termination time to provide a buffer between when the instance is released from the cluster and when it's dropped from the pool. This is helpful to ensure that idle instances remain available for subsequent jobs.
- Set the Max Capacity based on anticipated usage. This sets the ceiling for the maximum number of used and idle instances in the pool. Set the maximum capacity only if there is a strict instance quota or budget constraint.

Pre-populate pools

To benefit fully from pools, user should pre-populate newly created pools. Set the *Min Idle* instances greater than zero in the pool configuration. This is to ensure than Pool have available instances for the job.

If user wants to set this value to zero, use a starter job to ensure that newly created pools have available instances for clusters to access. With the starter job approach, schedule a job to run before jobs or users start using clusters. After the job finishes, the instances used for the job are released back to the pool. Set *Min Idle* instance setting to 0 and set the *Idle Instance Auto Termination* time high enough to ensure that idle instances remain available for subsequent jobs.

Using a starter job allows the pool instances to spin up, populate the pool, and remain available for job or interactive clusters.

Create a Pool

To create a pool using the UI:
- Click Compute in the sidebar.
- Click the Pools tab.
- Click the Create Pool button.
- Specify the pool configuration.
- Click the Create button.

To attach a cluster to a pool using the cluster creation UI, select the pool from the Driver Type or Worker Type dropdown while configuring the cluster. Available pools are listed at the top of each dropdown list. User can use the same pool or different pools for the driver node and worker nodes.

Minimum Idle Instances

When user creates a pool, in order to control its size, user can set three parameters: minimum idle instances, maximum capacity, and idle instance auto termination.

The minimum number of instances the pool keeps idle. These instances do not terminate, regardless of the auto termination settings. If a cluster consumes idle instances from the pool, Azure Databricks provisions additional instances to maintain the minimum.

Maximum Capacity

The maximum number of instances the pool can provision. If a cluster using the pool requests more instances than this number during autoscaling, the request fails with an INSTANCE_POOL_MAX_CAPACITY_FAILURE error. This configuration is *optional*. This is preferred if user have instance quota, or user needs to cap cost.

Idle Instance Auto Termination

The time in minutes that instances can be idle before being terminated by the pool.

Instance types

User defines instance type when creating a pool. A pool's instance type cannot be edited. Clusters attached to a pool use the same instance type for the driver and worker nodes. Based on use cases, such as memory-intensive or compute-intensive workloads, user can choose different families of instance types.

Pool tags

Pool tags allow to easily monitor the cost of cloud resources used by various groups in organization. User can specify tags as key-value pairs when user creates a pool.

Databricks applies three default tags to each pool: *Vendor*, *DatabricksInstancePoolId*, and *DatabricksInstancePoolCreatorId*. User can also add custom tags while creating a pool. User can add up to 41 custom tags. Pool-backed clusters inherit default and custom tags from the pool configuration.

To add additional tags to the pool, navigate to the *Tabs* tab at the bottom of the *Create Pool* page. Click the *+ Add* button, then enter the key-value pair.

Autoscaling local storage

Azure Databricks automatically enables autoscaling local storage on all Azure Databricks pools.

With autoscaling local storage, Azure Databricks monitors the amount of free disk space available on pool's instances. If an instance runs too low on disk, a new managed disk is attached automatically before it runs out of disk space. Managed disks are never detached from a virtual machine if it is part of a pool. The managed disks attached to a virtual machine are detached only when the virtual machine is returned to cloud provider.

Spot instances

To save cost, user can choose to use spot instances by checking the *All Spot* radio button. Clusters in the pool will launch with spot instances for all nodes, driver, and worker. If spot instances are evicted due to unavailability, on-demand instances do not replace evicted instances.

Delete a pool

Deleting a pool terminates the pool's idle instances and removes its configuration. If user deletes the pool then

- Running clusters attached to the pool continue to run but cannot allocate instances during resize or up-scaling.
- Terminated clusters attached to the pool will fail to start.

Databricks Container Services

Databricks Container Services lets us specify a Docker image while creating a cluster. Some examples use cases include:
- Library customization: User have full control over the system libraries user wants installed.
- Golden container environment: Docker image is a locked down environment that will never change.

- Docker CI/CD integration: User can integrate Azure Databricks with Docker CI/CD pipelines.

User can also use Docker images to create custom deep learning environments on clusters with GPU devices.

To launch cluster using UI:
- On the Create Cluster page, specify a Databricks Runtime Version that supports Databricks Container Services.
- Under Advanced options, select the Docker tab.
- Select Use your own Docker container.
- In the Docker Image URL field, enter custom Docker image.
- Docker image URL examples:

  Docker Hub : <organization>/<repository>:<tag>(e.g.databricksruntime/standard:latest)
  Azure Container Registry: <your-registry-name>.azurecr.io/<repository-name>:<tag>

Single Node clusters

A Single Node cluster is a cluster consisting of an Apache Spark driver and no Spark workers. A Single Node cluster supports Spark jobs and all Spark data sources, including Delta Lake. A Standard cluster requires a minimum of one Spark worker to run Spark jobs. Single Node clusters are helpful for:

- Single-node machine learning workloads that use Spark to load and save data.
- Lightweight exploratory data analysis

To create a Single Node cluster, select the *Single Node* button while configuring a cluster. A Single Node cluster has the following properties:

- Runs Spark locally.
- The driver acts as both master and worker, with no worker nodes.

A Single Node cluster has the following limitations:

- Large-scale data processing will exhaust the resources on a Single Node cluster. For these workloads, Databricks recommends using a Multi Node cluster.
- Single Node clusters are not designed to be shared.
- Single Node clusters are not compatible with process isolation.
- GPU scheduling is not enabled on Single Node clusters.

Debugging with the Apache Spark UI

There are different debugging options available to peek at the internals of Apache Spark application. The three important places to look are:

- Spark UI
- Driver logs

- Executor logs

Spark UI

Once the job is started, the Spark UI shows information about what's happening in the application. To get to the Spark UI, click the attached cluster.

Streaming tab

Once user gets to the Spark UI, user will see a Streaming tab if a streaming job is running in this cluster. If there is no streaming job running in this cluster, this tab will not be visible. Skip to Driver logs to learn how to check for exceptions that might have happened while starting the streaming job.

The first thing to look for in this page is to check if streaming application is receiving any input events from source.

Processing time

Processing Time graph helps to understand the performance of streaming job. As a general rule of thumb, it is good if user can process each batch within 80% of batch processing time e.g., if the batch interval is 2 seconds and the average processing time is 450ms, which is well under the batch interval. If the average processing time is closer or greater than the batch interval, then user will have a streaming application that will start queuing up resulting in backlog. The backlog can soon bring down streaming job eventually.

Completed batches

The end of the page displays details about the last 1000 batches that completed. From the table, user can get the numbers of events processed for each batch and their processing time. User can click the batch link to get more details.

Job details page

The job details page shows a DAG visualization. This is a very useful to understand the order of operations and dependencies for every batch. At the bottom of the page, user will also find the list of jobs that were executed for this batch. User can click the links in the description to drill further into the task level execution.

Driver logs

Driver logs are helpful for 2 purposes:
- Exceptions: Sometimes, User may not see the Streaming Tab in the Spark UI. This is because the Streaming job was not started because of some exception. User can drill into the Driver logs to look at the stack trace of the exception.
- Prints: Any print statements as part of the DAG shows up in the logs too.

Executor logs

Executor logs are sometimes helpful if user would like to see the logs for specific tasks. From the task details page, user can get the executor where the task was run. Once user has executor name, user can go to the clusters UI page, click the nodes, and then the master. The master page lists all the workers. User can choose the worker where the suspicious task was run and then get to the log4j output.

Handling large queries in interactive workflows

A challenge with interactive data workflows is handling large queries. These queries can be extremely slow, saturate cluster resources, and make it difficult for others to share the same cluster.

Query Watchdog is a process that prevents queries from monopolizing cluster resources by examining the most common causes of large queries and terminating queries that pass a threshold.

To enable Query Watchdog, set the following property:

```
spark.conf.set("spark.databricks.queryWatchdog.enabled", true)
```

To a prevent a query from creating too many output rows for the number of input rows, user can configure the maximum number of output rows as a multiple of the number of input rows. In this example shown below user use a ratio of 1000 (the default).

```
spark.conf.set("spark.databricks.queryWatchdog.outputRatioThreshold", 1000L)
```

The above configuration declares that any given task should never produce more than 1000 times the number of input rows.

Query Watchdog also saves time by fast failing a query that would have never completed. This is achieved through *minTimeSecs* & *minOutputRows* properties. *minTimeSecs* specifies the minimum time a given task in a query must run before cancelling it. *minOutputRows* specifies the minimum number of output rows for a task in that query.

User can set `minTimeSecs` to a higher value if user wants to give it a chance to produce a large number of rows per task.

User can set `spark.databricks.queryWatchdog.minOutputRows` to ten million if user wants to stop a query only after a task in that query has produced ten million rows. This is set through as shown below:

```
spark.conf.set("spark.databricks.queryWatchdog.minTimeSecs", 10L)
spark.conf.set("spark.databricks.queryWatchdog.minOutputRows", 100000L)
```

Query Watchdog should be enabled for ad hoc analytics clusters where SQL analysts and data scientists are sharing a given cluster and an administrator needs to make sure that queries "play nicely" with one another. It is recommended to disable Query Watchdog for all but ad hoc analytics clusters.

Databricks notebooks

Notebook is a common tool for developing code and presenting results. It is primary tool for creating data engineering workflows and collaborating with colleagues. Databricks notebooks provide real-time co-authoring in multiple languages, automatic versioning, and built-in data visualizations.

Create a Notebook

User can create a new notebook in any folder (for example, in the *Shared* folder) following these steps:

- In the sidebar, click *Workspace*.
- Right-click on the name of any folder and select *Create > Notebook*. A blank notebook opens in the workspace.

To change the title of an open notebook, click the title and edit inline or click *File > Rename.*

To view notebooks attached to a cluster, click on *Notebooks* tab on the cluster details page. The tab also displays the status of the notebook, along with the last time a command was run from the notebook.

Develop code in Databricks notebooks

Code or SQL statements are written in a notebook cell. Use Ctrl+Shift+Enter to execute the code of cell. If user wants to run only the part of the code in cell, select that piece of code and use Ctrl+Shift+Enter to run the selected text.

Run selected text   Python ˅

File   Edit   View   Run   Help   Last edit was now   Give feedback

Cmd 1

```
def power(n, m):
    return n ** m

power(3, 4)

print("End result is", power(5, 6))
```

Out[6]: 81

Version history

Azure Databricks notebooks maintain a history of notebook versions, allowing user to view and restore previous snapshots of the notebook. User can perform the following actions on versions: add comments, restore and delete versions, and clear version history.

To access notebook versions, select *File > Version history*.

To add a comment to the latest version, Click the version and click on Save now. In the Save Notebook Revision dialog, enter a comment and click on Save. The notebook version is saved with the entered comment.

To restore a version, Click the version which user wants to restore and click *"Restore this version"*. Click Confirm. The selected version becomes the latest version of the notebook.

To delete a version entry, Click the version that user wants to delete and click the trash icon. Click *Yes, erase* and the selected version is deleted from the history.

To clear the version history for a notebook, Select *File > Clear version history*. Click Yes, clear. The notebook version history is cleared.

Set default language

The default language for the notebook appears next to the notebook name.

To change the default language, click the language button and select the new language from the dropdown menu. To ensure that existing commands continue to work, commands of the previous default language are automatically prefixed with a language magic command. The language magic command format is %<language>. The supported magic commands are: %python, %r , %scala, and %sql.

By default, cells use the default language of the notebook. User can override the default language in a cell by clicking the language button and selecting a language from the dropdown menu.

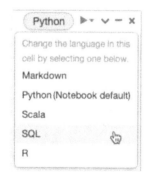

Notebooks also support a few auxiliary magic commands:

- %sh: Allows to run shell code in notebook.

- **%fs:** Allows to use dbutils filesystem commands e.g, to run the dbutils.fs.ls command to list files. User can specify %fs ls instead.
- **%md:** Allows to include various types of documentation, including text, images, and mathematical formulas and equations.

Link to other notebooks

User can link to other notebooks or folders using relative paths. Specify the `href` attribute of an anchor tag as the relative path, starting with a $

<a href="$./myFolder2/myNotebook2">Link to nested notebook</a>

Compute resources for notebooks

User can run a notebook on a Databricks cluster, or, for SQL commands, user also have the option to use a SQL warehouse, a type of compute that is optimized for SQL analytics.

To attach a notebook to a cluster, click the compute selector in the notebook toolbar and select a cluster from the dropdown menu. The menu shows a selection of clusters that user have used recently or that are currently running.

To select from all available clusters, click *More...*. Click on the cluster name to display a dropdown menu and select an existing cluster.

Attach to an existing compute resource   ✕

⦿ General cluster   ◯ SQL Warehouse

🔍 ⦿ | Q1 analysis cluster

⦿	Shared Test Cluster	DBR 12.2 LTS
⦿	Shared Test Cluster 2	DBR 12.2 LTS
⦿	Q1 analysis cluster	DBR 12.2 LTS
⦿	Forecasting Shared	DBR 12.1
◼	Spark Connect Shared Cluster	DBR 12.2 LTS

Summary

1 Driver	64 GB Memory, 16 Cores
Runtime	12.2.x-scala2.12

`Unity Catalog`
`3 DBU/h`

Create new resource   Cancel   **Attach**

User can also create a new cluster by selecting *Create new resource...* from the dropdown menu.

To Use a notebook with a SQL warehouse, select "SQL Warehouse" from the above image. When a notebook is attached to a SQL warehouse, user can run SQL and markdown cells. All other cells (Python, R, or other languages) are ignored.

To detach a notebook from a compute resource, click the compute selector in the notebook toolbar and hover over the attached cluster or SQL warehouse in the list to display a side menu. From the side menu, select *Detach*.

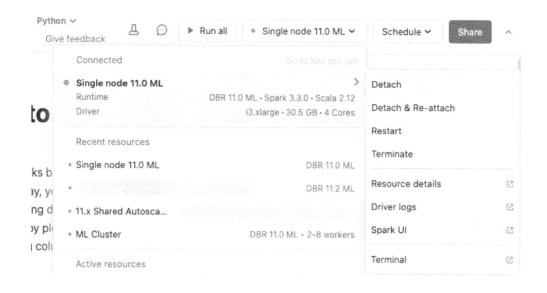

User can also detach notebooks from a cluster using the **Notebooks** tab on the cluster details page. When user detaches a notebook, the execution context is removed and all computed variable values are cleared from the notebook.

It is recommended to detach unused notebooks from clusters. This frees up memory space on the driver.

Schedule Notebook Job

User can create and manage notebook jobs directly in the notebook UI. If a notebook is already assigned to one or more jobs, user can create and manage schedules for those jobs. If a notebook is not assigned to a job, user can create a job and a schedule to run the notebook.

To schedule a notebook job, click Schedule button at the top right. If no jobs exist for this notebook, the Schedule dialog appears.

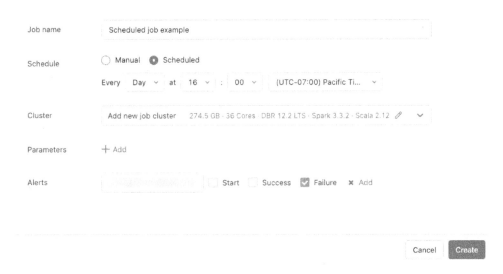

If jobs already exist for the notebook, the Jobs List dialog appears. User can still add a schedule by clicking on "Add a schedule" button in the Job list dialog.

In the Schedule dialog:

- Select *Manual* to run job only when manually triggered or *scheduled* to define a schedule for running the job. If user selects *scheduled*, use the dropdowns to specify the frequency, time, and time zone.
- In the *Cluster* drop-down, select the cluster to run the task.
- If user have *Allow Cluster Creation* permissions, by default the job runs on a new job cluster. If user does not have *Allow Cluster Creation* permissions, by default the job runs on the cluster that the notebook is attached to. If the notebook is not attached to a cluster, user must select a cluster from the *Cluster* drop-down.
- Optionally, enter any *Parameter* to pass to the job. Specify the key and value of each parameter. Through notebook widget, user can capture these parameters values in notebook.

- Optionally, specify email addresses to receive *Alerts* on job events.

Export and import Databricks Notebooks

Databricks can import and export notebooks in the following formats:
- Source file: A file containing only source code statements with the extension. scala, .py, .sql, or .r.
- HTML: An Azure Databricks notebook with the extension .html.
- Databricks .dbc archive.
- IPython notebook: A Jupyter notebook with the extension ipynb.
- RMarkdown: An R Markdown document with the extension Rmd.

To import a notebook.,
- Click Workspace in the sidebar.
- Right-click on a folder and select Import.
- Specify the URL or browse to a file.
- Click import.

If user chooses a single notebook, it is exported in the current folder. If user choose a DBC or ZIP archive, its folder structure is recreated in the current folder and each notebook is imported.

To export a notebook, select *File > Export* in the notebook toolbar and select the export format.

To export all folders in a workspace folder as a ZIP archive:

- Click Workspace in the sidebar.
- Right-click the folder and select Export. Select the export format for export.

When user exports a notebook as HTML, IPython notebook (.ipynb), or archive (DBC), and if user has not cleared the command outputs, the outputs are included in the export.

To clear the notebook state and outputs, select one of the Clear options at the bottom of the Run menu.

Share a notebook

To share a notebook with a co-worker, click Notebook header share button at the top of the notebook. The permissions dialog opens, which user can use to select who to share the notebook with and what level of access they have.

Databricks widgets

Input widgets allow user to add parameters to notebooks and dashboards. Databricks widgets are best for:
- Building a notebook or dashboard that is re-executed with different parameters.
- Quickly exploring results of a single query with different parameters

There are 4 types of widgets:
- text: Input a value in a text box.

- dropdown: Select a value from a list of provided values.
- combobox: Combination of text and dropdown. Select a value from a provided list or input one in the text box.
- multiselect: Select one or more values from a list of provided values.

Running the below python command creates widgets for each of the command.

```
dbutils.widgets.dropdown("state", "CA", ["CA", "IL", "MI", "NY", "OR", "VA"])
dbutils.widgets.text("database", "customers_dev")
```

The below image shows the widget created after execution of the above commands.

database	state
customers_dev	NY ⌄

The widget values can be retrieved using the below command.

```
dbutils.widgets.get("state")
dbutils.widgets.get("database")
```

Run a Databricks notebook from another notebook

A notebook can be called from another notebook using %run or dbutils.notebook.run() command.

User can use *%run* to modularize code, for example by putting supporting functions in a separate notebook. When user use %run, the called notebook is immediately executed and the functions and variables defined in it become available in the calling notebook.

The *dbutils.notebook* API is a complement to *%run* because it lets user pass parameters to and return values from a notebook. For example, user can get a list of files in a directory and pass the names to another notebook. User can also create if-then-else workflows based on return values or call other notebooks using relative paths. Widget parameter can be passed using %run, but user can't get the return value. Unlike %run, the *dbutils.notebook.run()* method starts a new job to run the notebook.

```
statusval=dbutils.notebook.run("notebook-name", 60, {"argument": "data", "argument2": "data2", ...})
```

In the above code, timeout value is 60 seconds. The return value from the execution will be stored in statusval variable. To implement this, dev should also implement exit() method in calling notebook. The exit value will stop the further execution and return the value of variable put in this. The below code should be implemented in calling notebook to return the value of status variable.

```
dbutils.notebook.exit("statusval")
```

Unit testing for notebooks

Unit testing is used to improve the quality and consistency of notebooks' code. Unit testing is an approach to testing self-contained units of code, such as function. This helps to find problems with code faster. There are a few common approaches for organizing functions and their unit tests with notebooks.

Store functions and their unit tests outside of notebooks.
The benefit of this approach is that user can call these functions with and outside of notebooks. Test frameworks are better designed to run tests outside of notebooks. The challenge is that this approach also increases the number of files to track and maintain.

Store functions in one notebook and their unit tests in a separate notebook
The benefit of this approach is that these functions are easier to reuse across notebooks. The challenge is that the number of notebooks to track and maintain increases. These functions cannot be used outside of notebooks.

Store functions and their unit tests within the same notebook
The benefit of this approach is that functions and their unit tests are stored within a single notebook for easier tracking and maintenance. The challenge is that these functions can be more difficult to reuse across notebooks. These functions cannot be used outside of notebooks.

For Python and R notebooks, Databricks recommends storing functions and their unit tests outside of notebooks. For Scala notebooks, Databricks recommends including functions in one notebook and their unit tests in a separate notebook.

For SQL notebooks, Databricks recommends that user stores functions as SQL user-defined functions (SQL UDFs) in schemas (databases). User can then call these SQL UDFs and their unit tests from SQL notebooks.

Sample unit test functions be:
- Whether a table exists in a database.
- Whether a column exists in a table.
- How many rows exist in a column for a value within that column.

To get the best unit testing results, a function should return a single predictable outcome and be of a single data type.

The below function returns how many rows exists in a column.

```
def numRowsInColumnForValue(dataFrame, columnName, columnValue):
 df = dataFrame.filter(col(columnName) == columnValue)
 return df.count()
```

User can create test function to test this feature. In the test notebook, pytest library must be installed and using the below code, this functionality can be tested. The df, columnName and columnValue variables value should be defined in notebook before call the below function.

```
import pytest
def test_numRowsInColumnForValue():
  assert numRowsInColumnForValue(df, columnName, columnValue) > 0
```

pytest looks for .py files whose names start with test_ (or end with _test) to test. Similarly, by default, pytest looks inside of these files for functions whose names start with test_ to test. So, the test notebook name should start with test_ or end with _test. The function inside the notebook should start with test_.

To install pytest, run the below command at first cell of notebook.

```
%pip install pytest
```

Databricks Workflows

Databricks Workflows orchestrates data processing, machine learning, and analytics pipelines in the Azure Databricks Lakehouse Platform. Workflows has fully managed orchestration services integrated with the Azure Databricks platform, including Databricks Jobs to run non-interactive code in Databricks workspace and Delta Live Tables to build reliable and maintainable ETL pipelines.

Workflow is orchestrated by an Databricks job.

Databricks Jobs

An Databricks job is a way to run data processing and analysis applications. Job can consist of a single task or can be a large, multi-task workflow with complex dependencies. Databricks manages the task orchestration, cluster management, monitoring, and error reporting for jobs. User can run jobs immediately, periodically through an easy-to-use scheduling system, whenever new files arrive in an external location, or continuously to ensure an instance of the job is always running. Jobs can be run interactively in the notebook UI. User can create and run a job using the Jobs UI, the Databricks CLI, or by invoking the Jobs API.

A job is composed of one or more tasks. Job tasks can be created that run notebooks, JARS, Delta Live Tables pipelines, or Python, Scala, Spark submit, and Java applications. Job tasks can also orchestrate Databricks SQL queries, alerts and dashboards to create analyses and visualizations.

User can also add a task to a job that runs a different job. This feature allows to break a large process into multiple smaller jobs or create generalized modules that can be reused by multiple jobs. User can control the execution order of tasks by specifying dependencies between the tasks. User can configure tasks to run in sequence or parallel.

Databricks clusters and SQL warehouses provide the computation resources for jobs. User can run jobs with a job cluster, an all-purpose cluster, or a SQL warehouse.

- A job cluster is a dedicated cluster for job or individual job tasks. A job can use a job cluster that's shared by all tasks, or user can configure a cluster for individual tasks when user creates or edits a task. A job cluster is created when the job or task starts and is terminated when the job or task ends.
- An all-purpose cluster is a shared cluster that is manually started and terminated and can be shared by multiple users and jobs.

To optimize resource usage, Databricks recommends using a job cluster for jobs. To reduce the time spent waiting for cluster startup, consider using an all-purpose cluster.

Databricks Jobs and Delta Live Tables

Delta Live Tables is a framework that simplifies ETL and streaming data processing. Delta Live Tables provides efficient ingestion of data with built-in support for Auto Loader, SQL and Python interfaces. User defines the transformations to perform on data, and Delta Live Tables manages task orchestration, cluster management, monitoring, data quality, and error handling.

Databricks Jobs and Delta Live Tables provide a comprehensive framework for building and deploying end-to-end data processing and analysis workflows. Use Delta Live Tables for all ingestion and transformation of data. Use Databricks Jobs to orchestrate workloads composed of a single task or multiple data processing and analysis tasks in the Lakehouse platform, including Delta Live Tables ingestion and transformation.

As a workflow orchestration system, Databricks Jobs supports:

- Running jobs on a triggered basis, for example, running a workflow on a schedule.
- Data analysis through SQL queries, machine learning and data analysis with notebooks, scripts, or external libraries, and so forth.
- Running a job composed of a single task, for example, running an Apache Spark job packaged in a JAR.

Create & Run Job

To create a Job, Click Workflows in the sidebar and click "Create Job". The **Tasks** tab appears with the create task dialog.

- Enter a name for the task in the *Task name* field.
- In the *Type* dropdown menu, select the type of task to run. The type of task can be notebook, python script, python wheel, jar, delta live table pipeline etc.

- Select the Source which indicate whether it is workspace or Git provider for file selection.
- Configure the cluster where the task runs. In the *Cluster* dropdown menu, select either *New job cluster* or *Existing All-Purpose Clusters*.
- To add dependent libraries, click + *Add* next to *Dependent libraries*. Dependent libraries will be installed on the cluster before the task runs.
- To pass parameters, click on Add and provide parameters.
- To optionally receive notifications for task start, success, or failure, click **+** *Add* next to *Emails*.
- To optionally configure a retry policy for the task, click **+** *Add* next to *Retries*.
- To optionally configure an expected duration or a timeout for the task, click **+** *Add* next to *Duration threshold*.
- Click on *Create to create* task.
- To add another task, click + icon in the DAG view.

To run the job immediately, click "Run Now" button.

User can use *Run Now with Different Parameters* to re-run a job with different parameters or different values for existing parameters.

Click ⌄ next to *Run Now* and select *Run Now with Different Parameters*. Enter the new parameters depending on the type of task and then click Run.

- *Notebook*: User can enter parameters as key-value pairs or a JSON object. The provided parameters are merged with the default parameters for the triggered run. User can use this dialog to set the values of widgets.
- *JAR* and *spark-submit*: User can enter a list of parameters or a JSON document.

Run a job as a service principal

By default, jobs run as the identity of the job owner. This means that the job assumes the permissions of the job owner. The job can only access data and Databricks objects that the job owner has permissions to access. User can change the identity that the job is running as to a service principal. Then, the job assumes the permissions of that service principal instead of the owner.

To change the *Run as* setting user should have either *Can Manage* or *Is Owner* permission on the job. To change the run as field, do the following:

- In the sidebar, click Workflows.
- In the Name column, click the job name.
- In the Job details side panel, click the pencil icon next to the Run as field.
- Search for and select the service principal.
- Click Save.

User can use a schedule to automatically run Databricks job at specified times and periods. To do this, select the Job, click it. Click Add trigger in the Job details panel and select Scheduled in Trigger type. To run continuous job, select *Continuous* in *Trigger type*.

To Trigger jobs when new files arrive, select *File arrival* in *Trigger type*. In Storage location, enter the URL of the external location or a subdirectory of the external location to monitor.

View and manage job runs

To view the list of jobs user has access to, click *Workflows* in the sidebar. The *Jobs* tab in the Workflows UI lists information about all available jobs, such as the creator of the job, the trigger for the job, if any, and the result of the last run.

User can view a list of currently running and recently completed runs for all jobs use has access to, including runs started by external orchestration tools such as Apache Airflow or Azure Data Factory. To view the list of recent job runs:

- Click Workflows in the sidebar.
- In the Name column, click a job name. The Runs tab appears with matrix and list views of active and completed runs.

The matrix view shows a history of runs for the job, including each job task. Some of the information displayed by runs list view are:

- The start time for the run.
- Whether the run was triggered by a job schedule or an API request, or was manually started.
- The status of the run like **Pending, Running, Skipped, Succeeded, Failed, Terminating** etc.
- Click ⋮ to stop an active run or delete a completed run.

Azure Databricks maintains a history of job runs for up to 60 days. If user needs to preserve job runs, Databricks recommends exporting results before they expire.

Share information between tasks in job

User can use task values to pass arbitrary parameters between tasks in an Databricks job. Task values are passed using the taskValues subutility in Databricks Utilities. The taskValues subutility provides a simple API that allows tasks to output values that can be referenced in subsequent tasks. Each task can set and get multiple task values. Task values can be set and retrieved in Python notebooks.

The taskValues subutility provides two commands: dbutils.jobs.taskValues.set() to set a variable and dbutils.jobs.taskValues.get() to retrieve a value. Suppose there are two notebook tasks: Get_user_data and Analyze_user_data and want to pass user's name and age from the Get_user_data task to Analyze_user_data task. So, the below code should be executed in databrick notebook in the Get_user_data notebook.

```
dbutils.jobs.taskValues.set(key = 'name', value = 'Some User')
dbutils.jobs.taskValues.set(key = "age", value = 30)
```

Key is the task value and value is the value for this task value's key. The below code gets the values in second notebook.

```
dbutils.jobs.taskValues.get(taskKey = "Get_user_data", key = "age", default = 42, debugValue =
0)
dbutils.jobs.taskValues.get(taskKey = "Get_user_data", key = "name", default = "Jane Doe")
```

Here taskKey is the name of the job task setting the value. If the command cannot find this task, a ValueError is raised.

Pass context about job runs into job tasks.

User can pass the context about a job run, such as the run ID or the job's start time. The below templated variables into a job task will pass Job Id. This variable should be passed as part of the task's parameters.

```
{
   "MyJobID": "{{job_id}}"
}
```

Run tasks conditionally in an Databricks job

User can configure tasks in an Databricks job to only run when specific conditions are met. User can use the *Run if* condition to run a task even when some or all its dependencies have failed, allowing job to recover from failures and continue running.

User can configure a *Run if* condition when user edits a task with one or more dependencies. To add the condition to the task, select the condition from the *Run if* dropdown menu in the task configuration. The *Run if* condition is evaluated after all task dependencies have been completed. User can also add a *Run if* condition when user adds a new task with one or more dependencies.

User can add the following *Run if* conditions to a task:
- All succeeded: All dependencies have run and succeeded. This is the default condition to run a task. The task is marked as failed if the condition is not met.
- At least one succeeded: At least one dependency has succeeded. The task is marked as failed if the condition is not met.
- None failed: None of the dependencies failed, and at least one dependency was run. The task is marked as failed if the condition is not met.
- All done: All dependencies have completed.
- At least one failed: At least one dependency failed. The task is marked as Excluded if the condition is not met.

- All failed: All dependencies have failed. The task is marked as Excluded if the condition is not met.

Databricks Jobs determines whether a job run was successful based on the outcome of the job's *leaf tasks*. A leaf task is a task that has no downstream dependencies. A job run can have one of three outcomes:
- Succeeded: All tasks were successful.
- Succeeded with failures: Some tasks failed, but all leaf tasks were successful.
- Failed: One or more leaf tasks failed.

Failures handled for continuous jobs

Databricks Jobs uses an *exponential backoff* scheme to manage continuous jobs with multiple consecutive failures. Exponential backoff allows continuous jobs to run without pausing and return to a healthy state when recoverable failures occur.

When a continuous job exceeds the allowable threshold for consecutive failures, the following describes how subsequent job runs are managed:

- The job is restarted after a retry period set by the system.
- If the next job run fails, the retry period is increased, and the job is restarted after this new retry period.
  - For each subsequent job run failure, the retry period is increased again, up to a maximum retry period set by the system. There is no limit on the number of retries.
  - If the job run completes successfully and starts a new run, or if the run exceeds a threshold without failure, the job is considered healthy, and the backoff sequence resets.

Storage

Databricks uses a shared responsibility model to create, configure, and access block storage volumes and object storage locations in user's cloud account. Loading data to or saving data with Databricks results in files stored in either cloud block storage or object storage.

Cloud Object storage or blob storage refers to storage containers that maintain data as objects. Some object storage offerings include features like versioning and lifecycle management. Object storage has the following benefits:

- High availability, durability, and reliability.
- Lower cost for storage compared to most other storage options.
- Infinitely scalable (limited by the total amount of storage available in a given region of the cloud).

Most cloud-based data lakes are built on top of open-source data formats in cloud object storage. In almost all cases, the data files user interacts with using Apache Spark on Azure Databricks are stored in cloud object storage.

Block storage or disk storage refer to storage volumes that correspond to traditional hard disk drives (HDDs) or solid-state drives (SSDs). All virtual machines (VMs) require an attached block storage volume.

When user turn on compute resources as part of cluster, Databricks configures and deploys VMs and attaches block storage volumes. This block storage is used for storing ephemeral data files for the lifetime of the compute. These files include the operating system and installed libraries. While Apache Spark uses block storage in the background for efficient parallelization and data loading, most code run on Databricks does not directly save or load data to block storage. The data is mostly saved to cloud object storage.

Databrick can connect to cloud storage e.g. Azure Data Lake Storage Gen2 using Unity Catalog external locations and Azure managed identities. User can also set Spark properties to configure an Azure credentials to access Azure storage.

Connect to Azure Data Lake Storage Gen2 with Unity Catalog

Unity Catalog supports Azure Data Lake Storage Gen2. External locations and storage credentials allow Unity Catalog to read and write data in Azure Data Lake Storage Gen2. A storage credential is used for authentication to Azure Data Lake Storage Gen2. It can be either an Azure managed identity or a service principal. Databricks recommends using an Azure managed identity. An external location is an object that combines a cloud storage path with a storage credential.

The Databricks user who creates the external location in Unity Catalog must be a metastore admin or a user with the CREATE EXTERNAL LOCATION privilege.

82

After user creates an external location in Unity Catalog, user can grant the following permissions on it:

- CREATE TABLE
- READ FILES
- WRITE FILES

These permissions enable Azure Databricks users to access data in Azure Data Lake Storage Gen2. Use the fully qualified ABFS URI to access data secured with Unity Catalog.

To access the external location, user can use the ABFS path: -

```
dbutils.fs.ls("abfss://container@storageAccount.dfs.core.windows.net/external-location/path/to/data")
```

To read the file from the external location:

```
spark.read.format("parquet").load("abfss://container@storageAccount.dfs.core.windows.net/external-location/path/to/data")
```

To Save the file to this external location:

```
df.write.format("parquet").save("abfss://container@storageAccount.dfs.core.windows.net/external-location/path/to/new-location")
```

To create table in unity catalog:

```
CREATE TABLE <catalog>.<schema>.<table-name>
(
  <column-specification>
)
LOCATION 'abfss://<bucket-path>/<table-directory>'
```

The above SQL code will create the table in unity catalog which points to external location.

Connect to Blob Storage

The following credentials can be used to access Azure Data Lake Storage Gen2 or Blob Storage.

- OAuth 2.0 with an Azure service principal: Databricks recommends using Azure service principals to connect to Azure storage. User can set Spark properties to configure Azure credentials to access Azure storage.

```
service_credential = dbutils.secrets.get(scope="<secret-scope>",key="<service-credential-key>")

spark.conf.set("fs.azure.account.auth.type.<storage-account>.dfs.core.windows.net", "OAuth")
```

```
spark.conf.set("fs.azure.account.oauth.provider.type.<storage-account>.dfs.core.windows.net",
"org.apache.hadoop.fs.azurebfs.oauth2.ClientCredsTokenProvider")
spark.conf.set("fs.azure.account.oauth2.client.id.<storage-account>.dfs.core.windows.net", "<application-
id>")
spark.conf.set("fs.azure.account.oauth2.client.secret.<storage-account>.dfs.core.windows.net",
service_credential)
spark.conf.set("fs.azure.account.oauth2.client.endpoint.<storage-account>.dfs.core.windows.net",
"https://login.microsoftonline.com/<directory-id>/oauth2/token")
```

Replace

- <secret-scope> with the Databricks secret scope name.
- <service-credential-key> with the name of the key containing the client secret.
- <storage-account> with the name of the Azure storage account.
- <application-id> with the Application (client) ID for the Azure Active Directory application.
- <directory-id> with the Directory (tenant) ID for the Azure Active Directory application.

- Shared access signatures (SAS): User can use storage SAS tokens to access Azure storage. With SAS, user can restrict access to a storage account using temporary tokens with fine-grained access control.

```
spark.conf.set("fs.azure.account.auth.type.<storage-account>.dfs.core.windows.net", "SAS")
spark.conf.set("fs.azure.sas.token.provider.type.<storage-account>.dfs.core.windows.net",
"org.apache.hadoop.fs.azurebfs.sas.FixedSASTokenProvider")
spark.conf.set("fs.azure.sas.fixed.token.<storage-account>.dfs.core.windows.net",
dbutils.secrets.get(scope="<scope>", key="<sas-token-key>"))
```

Replace
- <storage-account> with the Azure Storage account name.
- <scope> with the Azure Databricks secret scope name.
- <sas-token-key> with the name of the key containing the Azure storage SAS token.

- Account keys: User can use storage account access keys to manage access to Azure Storage. Storage account access keys provide full access to the configuration of a storage account, as well as the data.

```
spark.conf.set(
    "fs.azure.account.key.<storage-account>.dfs.core.windows.net",
    dbutils.secrets.get(scope="<scope>", key="<storage-account-access-key>"))
```

Replace
- <storage-account> with the Azure Storage account name.
- <scope> with the Azure Databricks secret scope name.
- <storage-account-access-key> with the name of the key containing the Azure storage account access key.

Once User has properly configured credentials to access Azure storage container, user can interact with resources in the storage account using URIs. Databricks recommends using the *abfss* driver for greater security.

spark.read.load("abfss://<container-name>@<storage-account-name>.dfs.core.windows.net/<path-to-data>

Using SQL to load a csv file:

CREATE TABLE <database-name>.<table-name>;

COPY INTO <database-name>.<table-name>
FROM 'abfss://container@storageAccount.dfs.core.windows.net/path/to/folder'
FILEFORMAT = CSV
COPY_OPTIONS ('mergeSchema' = 'true');

Databricks recommends using an Azure service principal or a SAS token to connect to Azure storage instead of account keys. Databricks recommends using secret scopes for storing all credentials. User can grant users, service principals, and groups in workspace access to read the secret scope. This protects the Azure credentials while allowing users to access Azure storage.

Libraries

To make third-party or custom code available to notebooks and jobs running on clusters, user needs to install relevant library. Libraries can be written in Python, Java, Scala, and R. User can perform library tasks through Workspace UI, CLI or Libraries API.

User can install libraries in three modes: cluster-installed, notebook-scoped, and workspace.

- Cluster libraries: Cluster libraries can be used by all notebooks running on a cluster. User can install a cluster library directly from the following sources:
    - A public repository such as PyPI, Maven, or CRAN.
    - A cloud object storage location.
    - A workspace library in the DBFS root.
    - Uploading library files from local machine.
- Notebook-scoped libraries: Notebook-scoped libraries, available for Python and R, allow to install libraries and create an environment scoped to a notebook session. These libraries do not affect other notebooks running on the same cluster. Notebook scoped libraries do not persist and must be re-installed for each session.
- Workspace libraries: Workspace libraries serve as a local repository from which user can create cluster-installed libraries. A workspace library might be custom code created by user's organization or might be a particular version of an open-source library that user's organization has standardized on.

Workspace libraries

Workspace libraries serve as a local repository from which user creates cluster-installed libraries. A workspace library might be custom code created by user's organization or might be a particular version of an open-source library that user's organization has standardized on.

To create workspace library:

- Right-click the workspace folder where user wants to store the library.
- Select *Create > Library*. The Create Library dialog appears.
- Select the *Library Source* and select Library type to install the library. The following are the library source options:
    - Upload a library
    - Reference an uploaded library
    - PyPI package
    - Maven package
    - CRAN package

Workspace libraries in the Shared folder are available to all users in a workspace, while workspace libraries in a user folder are available only to that user.

Upload a Jar, Python egg, or Python wheel

- In the Library Source button list, select Upload.

- Select Jar, Python Egg, or Python Whl.
- Optionally enter a library name.
- Drag Jar, Egg, or Whl to the drop box or click the drop box and navigate to a file. The file is uploaded to dbfs:/FileStore/jars.
- Click Create. The library status screen displays.

Reference an uploaded jar, Python egg, or Python wheel

User can create a new workspace library by referencing jar, egg, or wheel files stored in the DBFS root, on object storage, or with workspace files.

1. Select DBFS/ADLS in the Library Source button list.
2. Select Jar, Python Egg, or Python Whl.
3. Optionally enter a library name.
4. Specify the path to the library.
5. Click Create. The library status screen displays.

Install a workspace library onto a cluster

User must install a workspace library on a cluster before it can be used in a notebook or job.

To install workspace library:

- In the sidebar, click Compute.
- Click a cluster name.
- Click the Libraries tab.
- Click Install New.
- In the Library Source button list, select Workspace Library.
- Select a workspace library.
- Click Install.

Move a workspace library

Workspace folders provide convenience for discovering workspace libraries and managing ACLs. Moving a workspace library does not move files but can modify which users have access to the workspace library.

- Go to the workspace folder containing the library.
- Right-click the library name and select Move. A folder browser displays.
- Click the destination folder.
- Click Move.

Delete a workspace library

Before deleting a workspace library, user should uninstall it from all clusters. To delete a workspace library:

- Move the library to the Trash folder.
- Either permanently delete the library in the Trash folder or empty the Trash folder.

Cluster libraries

Cluster libraries can be used by all notebooks running on a cluster. In this, user should install a library for use with a specific cluster. When user install a library on a cluster, a notebook already attached to that cluster will not immediately see the new library. User must first detach and then reattach the notebook to the cluster.

To install a library on a cluster:
- Click Compute in the sidebar.
- Click a cluster name.
- Click the Libraries tab.
- Click Install New.
- The Install library dialog displays.
- Select one of the Library Source options, complete the instructions that appear, and then click Install.

Install libraries from a package repository

Azure Databricks provides tools to install libraries from PyPI, Maven, and CRAN package repositories.

For pyPI package installation, select *PyPI* in *Library Source* button list. Enter a PyPI package name. To install a specific version of a library, use this format for the library: `<library>==<version>` For example, `scikit-learn==0.19.1`.

Install libraries from object storage

User can store custom JAR and Python Whl libraries in cloud object storage and install these libraries in cluster. User installing the library should have appropriate permissions to object storage. It is recommended to configure all privileges related to library installation with read-only permissions. Databricks recommends using Azure service principals to manage access to libraries stored in Azure Data Lake Storage Gen2. To install a library stored in cloud object storage to a cluster, complete the following steps:

- Select a cluster from the list in the clusters UI.
- Select the Libraries tab.
- Select the DBFS/ADLS option.
- Provide the full URI path to the library object (for example, abfss://container-name@storage-account-name.dfs.core.windows.net/path/to/library.whl).
- Click Install.

User can use **%pip** to install custom Python wheels stored in object storage scoped to a notebook isolated SparkSession. To use this method, user must either store libraries in publicly readable object storage or use a pre-signed URL. Jar libraries cannot be installed in the notebook. User must install Jar libraries at the cluster level.

Databricks Repos

Databricks Repos is a visual Git client and API in Azure Databricks. Databricks Repos provides source control for projects by integrating with Git providers.

In Databricks Repos, user can use Git functionality to:
- Clone, push to, and pull from a remote Git repository.
- Create and manage branches for development work, including merging, rebasing, and resolving conflicts.
- Create notebooks and edit notebooks and other files.
- Visually compare differences upon commit.

Databricks supports the following Git providers:
- GitHub and GitHub AE
- Bitbucket Cloud
- GitLab
- Azure DevOps

Databricks Repos also supports Bitbucket Server, GitHub Enterprise Server, and GitLab self-managed integration, if the server is internet accessible.

Databricks Repos use a personal access token (PAT) or an equivalent credential to authenticate with the Git provider. To use Repos, user first need to add Git PAT and Git provider username to Databricks.

To modify a public remote repository, or to clone or modify a private remote repository, user must have a Git provider username and personal access token with read and write permissions for the remote repository.

Connect to a GitHub repo using a personal access token

In GitHub, follow these steps to create a personal access token that allows access to the repositories:

- Login to GitHub portal
- In the upper-right corner of any page, click the profile photo, then click Settings.
- Click Developer settings shown the left side items.
- Click the Personal access tokens tab.
- Click the Generate new token button.
- Enter a token description.
- Select the repo scope and workflow scope and click the Generate token button. Workflow scope is needed in case the repository has GitHub Action workflows.

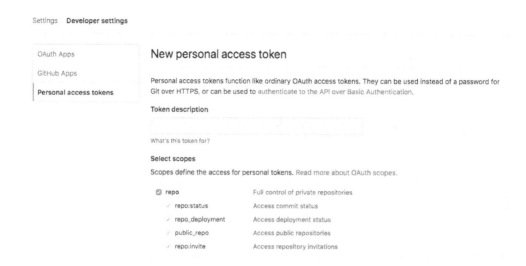

- Copy the token to clipboard. This token will be used in Databrick for connecting to Git.

Add or edit Git credentials in Databricks

- Open Databrick workspace
- Select the down arrow next to the account name at the top right of screen, and then select *User Settings*.
- Select the *Git Integration* tab.
- In the Git provider drop-down, select the provider's name.
- In the box provided, add Git user name or email.
- In the *Token* box, add a personal access token (PAT) or other credentials from Git provider (as done in the previous section)
- Databrick connection of Azure Devops, GitLab, Bitbucket can be done in similar way.

Git operation with repos

User can perform many Git operations with Databricks Repos.

Add a repo and connect remotely later

User can create a new repo in Databricks and add the remote Git repository URL later.

- To create a new repo not linked to a remote Git repository, click the Add Repo button. User can access Repo button through:
  Workspace→Repo→Right click on the user's mail id→Create→Repo.
  Deselect Create repo by cloning a Git repository, enter a name for the repo, and then click Create Repo.

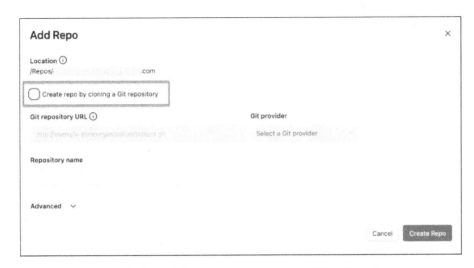

- When user is ready to add the Git repository URL, click the down arrow next to the repo name in the workspace to open the Repo menu, and select *Git...* to open the Git dialog.

- In the *Git repo URL* field, enter the URL for the remote repository and select the Git provider from the drop-down menu. Click **Save**.

Clone a repo connected to a remote repo

- In the sidebar, select *Workspace > Repos.*
- Click *Add Repo.*

- In the Add Repo dialog, select *Create repo by cloning a Git repository* and enter the repository URL
- Select Git provider from the drop-down menu, optionally change the name to use for the Databricks repo, and click *Create Repo.* The contents of the remote repository are cloned to the Databricks repo.

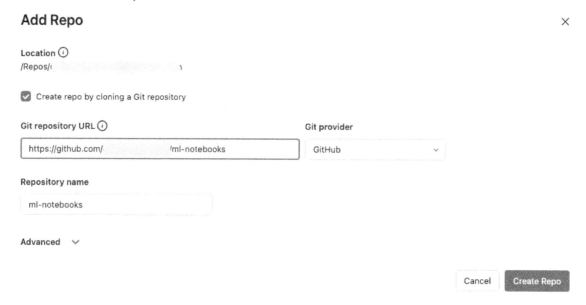

Access the Git dialog

User can access the Git dialog from a notebook or from the Databricks Repos browser.

- From a notebook, click the button next to the name of the notebook that identifies the current Git branch.

- From the Databricks Repos browser, click the button to the right of the repo name. User can also right-click the repo name and select *Git...* from the menu.

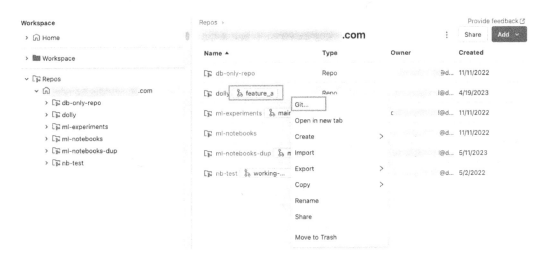

- To pull changes from the remote Git repository, click Pull button in the Git dialog. Notebooks and other files are updated automatically to the latest version in remote repository.

Rebase a branch on another branch

To rebase a branch on another branch:

- From the *Branch* menu in the Repos UI, select the branch user wants to rebase.
- Select *Rebase* from the menu as shown below.

- Select the branch to which user wants to rebase on. The rebase operation integrates changes from the branch user chooses here into the current branch.

Databricks File System (DBFS)

The Databricks File System (DBFS) is a distributed file system mounted into an Databricks workspace and available on Databricks clusters.

DBFS provides convenience by mapping cloud object storage URIs to relative paths.
- Allows user to interact with object storage using directory and file semantics instead of cloud-specific API commands.
- Allows user to mount cloud object storage locations.
- It simplifies the process of persisting files to object storage, allowing virtual machines and attached volume storage to be safely deleted on cluster termination.
- It provides a convenient location for storing init scripts, JARs, libraries, and configurations for cluster initialization.
- It provides a convenient location for checkpoint files created during model training.

Interact with files in cloud-based object storage

DBFS provides many options for interacting with files in cloud object storage:

- How to work with files on Azure Databricks
- List, move, copy, and delete files with Databricks Utilities
- Browse files in DBFS
- Upload files to DBFS with the UI
- Interact with DBFS files using the Databricks CLI
- Interact with DBFS files using the Databricks REST API

Mount object storage

Mounting object storage to DBFS allows users to access objects in object storage as if they were on the local file system. Mounted data does not work with Unity Catalog. Databricks recommends migrating away from using mounts.

Databricks mounts create a link between a workspace and cloud object storage, which enables user to interact with cloud object storage. Mounts work by creating a local alias under the /mnt directory that stores the following information:
- Location of the cloud object storage.
- Driver specifications to connect to the storage account or container.
- Security credentials required to access the data.

The syntax for mounting is:

```
dbutils.fs.mount(
  source: str,
  mount_point: str,
  encryption_type: Optional[str] = "",
  extra_configs: Optional[dict[str:str]] = None)
```

The source specifies the URI of the object storage. The mount_point specifies the local path in the /mnt directory. Some object storage sources support an optional encryption_type argument. For some access patterns, user can pass additional configuration specifications as a dictionary to extra_configs. Running the following code create a mount point.

```
configs = {"fs.azure.account.auth.type": "OAuth",
        "fs.azure.account.oauth.provider.type": "org.apache.hadoop.fs.azurebfs.oauth2.ClientCredsTokenProvider",
        "fs.azure.account.oauth2.client.id": "<application-id>",
        "fs.azure.account.oauth2.client.secret": dbutils.secrets.get(scope="<scope-name>",key="<service-credential-key-name>"),
        "fs.azure.account.oauth2.client.endpoint": "https://login.microsoftonline.com/<directory-id>/oauth2/token"}


dbutils.fs.mount(
  source = "abfss://<container-name>@<storage-account-name>.dfs.core.windows.net/",
  mount_point = "/mnt/<mount-name>",
  extra_configs = configs)
```

- <application-id> with the Application (client) ID for the Azure Active Directory application.
- <scope-name> with the Databricks secret scope name.
- <service-credential-key-name> with the name of the key containing the client secret.
- <directory-id> with the Directory (tenant) ID for the Azure Active Directory application.
- <container-name> with the name of a container in the ADLS Gen2 storage account.
- <storage-account-name> with the ADLS Gen2 storage account name.
- <mount-name> with the name of the intended mount point in DBFS.

To unmount a mount point, use the following command:

```
dbutils.fs.unmount("/mnt/<mount-name>")
```

DBFS root

The *DBFS root* is the default storage location for an Databricks workspace, provisioned as part of workspace creation in the cloud account containing the Databricks workspace.

DBFS is a file system used for interacting with data in cloud object storage, but the DBFS root is a cloud object storage location. DBFS is used to interact with the DBFS root, but they are distinct concepts, and DBFS has many applications beyond the DBFS root.

DBFS work with Unity Catalog

Unity Catalog introduces a number of new configurations and concepts that approach data governance entirely differently than DBFS.

Databricks recommends against using DBFS and mounted cloud object storage for most use cases in Unity Catalog-enabled Databricks workspaces. In some scenarios, user should use mounted cloud object storage.

The DBFS root is the default location for storing files associated with a number of actions performed in the Azure Databricks workspace, including creating managed tables in the workspace-scoped hive_metastore.

Clusters configured with Single User access mode have full access to DBFS, including all files in the DBFS root and mounted data. DBFS root and mounts are available in this access mode, making it the choice for ML workloads that need access to Unity Catalog datasets.

Databricks recommends using service principals with scheduled jobs and Single User access mode for production workloads that need access to data managed by both DBFS and Unity Catalog.

Shared access mode combines Unity Catalog data governance with Azure Databricks legacy table ACLs. Access to data in the *hive_metastore* is only available to users that have permissions explicitly granted.

Each Unity Catalog metastore has an object storage account configured by an Azure Databricks account administrator. Unity Catalog uses this location to store all data and metadata for Unity Catalog-managed tables.

It is possible to load existing storage accounts into Unity Catalog using external locations. For greatest security, Databricks recommends only loading storage accounts to external locations if all other storage credentials and access patterns have been revoked.

User should never load a storage account used as a DBFS root as an external location in Unity Catalog.

Default Location

Each Databricks workspace has several directories configured in the DBFS root storage container by default. Some of these directory's link to locations on the DBFS root, while others are virtual mounts.

- /Filestore: Data and libraries uploaded through the Azure Databricks UI go to the **/Filestore** location by default.
- /databricks-datasets: Databricks provides a number of open source datasets in this directory
- /databricks-results: **/databricks-results** stores files generated by downloading the full results of a query
- /databricks/init: This directory contains legacy global init scripts.
- /user/hive/warehouse: Azure Databricks stores managed tables in the hive_metastore here by default.

FileStore

FileStore is a special folder within DBFS where user can save files and have them accessible to web browser. User can use FileStore to:

- Save files, such as images and libraries.
- Save output files that user wants to download to local desktop.
- Upload CSVs and other data files your local desktop to process on Databricks.

To Save a file to FileStore, user can use **dbutils.fs.put** to write arbitrary text files to the **/FileStore** directory in DBFS:

```
dbutils.fs.put("/FileStore/my-stuff/my-file.txt", "This is a sample text file")
```

Browse files in DBFS

User can browse and search for DBFS objects using the DBFS file browser. A workspace admin user must enable the DBFS browser interface before user can use it. The steps are:

- Click Data/Catalog in the sidebar.
- Click the Browse DBFS button at the top of the page.

The browser displays DBFS objects.

Work with Files

User can work with files on DBFS, the local driver node of the cluster, cloud object storage, external locations, and in Databricks Repos. User can integrate other systems, but many of these do not provide direct file access to Databricks.

The DBFS root is the root path for Spark and DBFS commands. These include:
- Spark SQL
- DataFrames
- dbutils.fs
- %fs

Access files on the DBFS root

When using commands that default to the DBFS root, user can use the relative path or include dbfs:/. The commands will be:

Using SQL:

```
SELECT * FROM parquet.`<path>`;
SELECT * FROM parquet.`dbfs:/<path>`
```

Using Python:

```
df = spark.read.load("<path>")
df.write.save("<path>")
```

Optimization & Performance

Databricks provides many optimizations ranging from large-scale ETL processing to ad-hoc, interactive queries. Many of these optimizations take place automatically. User gets their benefits simply by using Databricks.

Databricks configures default configuration values that optimize most workloads. In some cases, changing configuration settings improves performance. Use the latest Databricks Runtime to leverage the newest performance enhancements.

Optimize performance with caching

Databricks uses disk caching to accelerate data reads by creating copies of remote Parquet data files in nodes' local storage. The data is cached automatically whenever a file has to be fetched from a remote location. Successive reads of the same data are then performed locally, which results in significantly improved reading speed. Cache is of two types:

- Disk cache
- Apache Spark cache

The Databricks disk cache differs from Apache Spark caching. Databricks recommends using automatic disk caching for most operations.

When the disk cache is enabled, data that must be fetched from a remote source is automatically added to the cache. This process is fully transparent and does not require any action. To preload data into the cache beforehand, user can use the CACHE SELECT command. When user uses the Spark cache, user must manually specify the tables and queries to cache.

The disk cache contains local copies of remote data. It can improve the performance of a wide range of queries, but cannot be used to store results of query. The Spark cache can store the result of any query data and data stored in formats other than Parquet (such as CSV, JSON, and ORC).

The data stored in the disk cache can be read and operated on faster than the data in the Spark cache. This is because the disk cache uses efficient decompression algorithms and outputs data in the optimal format for further processing. Disk caching does not use system memory. Due to the high read speeds of modern SSDs, the disk cache has no negative impact on its performance.

The following table summarizes the key differences between disk and Apache Spark caching:

Feature	disk cache	Apache Spark cache
Stored as	Local files on a worker node.	In-memory blocks, but it depends on storage level.
Applied to	Any Parquet table stored on ABFS and other file systems.	Any DataFrame or RDD.

Triggered	Automatically, on the first read (if cache is enabled).	Manually, requires code changes.
Evaluated	Lazily	Lazily
Availability	Can be enabled or disabled with configuration flags	Always available.

The disk cache automatically detects when data files are created, deleted, modified, or overwritten and updates its content accordingly. There is no need to explicitly invalidate cached data. Any stale entries are automatically invalidated and evicted from the cache.

To explicitly select a subset of data to be cached, use the following syntax:

CACHE SELECT column_name[column_name, ...] FROM [db_name.]table_name [WHERE boolean_expression]

The recommended way to use disk caching is to choose a worker type with SSD volumes when user configures the cluster. Such workers are enabled and configured for disk caching.

Databricks recommends that user choose cache-accelerated worker instance types for clusters. Such instances are configured optimally for the disk cache.

Configure disk usage

To configure how the disk cache uses the worker nodes' local storage, specify the following Spark configuration settings during cluster creation:

- *spark.databricks.io.cache.maxDiskUsage*: Disk space per node reserved for cached data in bytes
- *spark.databricks.io.cache.maxMetaDataCache*: Disk space per node reserved for cached metadata in bytes
- *spark.databricks.io.cache.compression.enabled*: Should the cached data be stored in compressed format.

Example configuration:

spark.databricks.io.cache.maxDiskUsage 50g
spark.databricks.io.cache.maxMetaDataCache 1g
spark.databricks.io.cache.compression.enabled false

Enable or disable the disk cache.

To enable and disable the disk cache, run the following code in scala. Disabling the cache does not result in dropping the data that is already in the local storage. Instead, it prevents queries from adding new data to the cache and reading data from the cache.

spark.conf.set("spark.databricks.io.cache.enabled", "[true | false]")

Dynamic file pruning

Dynamic file pruning, can significantly improve the performance of many queries on Delta Lake tables. Dynamic File Pruning (DFP), a new data-skipping technique, which can significantly improve queries with selective joins on non-partition columns on tables in Delta Lake, now enabled by default in Databricks Runtime.

Dynamic file pruning is controlled by the following Apache Spark configuration options:

- *spark.databricks.optimizer.dynamicFilePruning*: Default is true. When set to **false**, dynamic file pruning will not be in effect.
- *spark.databricks.optimizer.deltaTableSizeThreshold*: Default is 10,000,000,000 bytes (10 GB). Represents the minimum size (in bytes) of the Delta table on the probe side of the join required to trigger dynamic file pruning. If the probe side is not very large, it is probably not worthwhile to push down the filters and user can just simply scan the whole table.
- *spark.databricks.optimizer.deltaTableFilesThreshold*: It represents the number of files of the Delta table on the probe side of the join required to trigger dynamic file pruning. When the probe side table contains fewer files than the threshold value, dynamic file pruning is not triggered. If a table has only a few files, it is probably not worthwhile to enable dynamic file pruning.

Low shuffle merge

The MERGE command is used to perform simultaneous updates, insertions, and deletions from a Delta Lake table. Azure Databricks has an optimized implementation of MERGE that improves performance substantially for common workloads by reducing the number of shuffle operations.

Databricks low shuffle merge provides better performance by processing unmodified rows in a separate, more streamlined processing mode, instead of processing them together with the modified rows. As a result, the amount of shuffled data is reduced significantly, leading to improved performance. In low shuffle merge, the unmodified rows are instead processed without any shuffles, expensive processing, or other added overhead. This provides optimized performance.

Low shuffle merge tries to preserve the existing data layout of the unmodified records, including Z-order optimization on a best-effort basis. The updated or newly inserted data may not be optimal, so it may still be necessary to run the OPTIMIZE or OPTIMIZE ZORDER BY commands.

Low shuffle merge is enabled by default in Databricks Runtime 10.4 and above. In earlier supported Databricks Runtime versions it can be enabled by setting the configuration: *spark.databricks.delta.merge.enableLowShuffle* to true.

Delta Lake

Delta Lake is the optimized storage layer that provides the foundation for storing data and tables in the Databricks Lakehouse Platform. Delta Lake is open source software that store data as Parquet files with a file-based transaction log for ACID transactions.

Delta Lake is the default storage format for all operations on Databricks. Unless otherwise specified, all tables on Databricks are Delta tables. All tables on Databricks are Delta tables by default. Whether user is using Apache Spark DataFrames or SQL, user gets all the benefits of Delta Lake just by saving data to the lakehouse with default settings.

Delta Lake operations

Create a table

All tables created on Databricks use Delta Lake by default.

Using python:

```
# Load the data from its source.
df = spark.read.load("/databricks-datasets/learning-spark-v2/people/people.delta")


# Write the data to a table.
table_name = "people_data"
df.write.saveAsTable(table_name)
```

Using SQL:

```
DROP TABLE IF EXISTS people_data;


CREATE TABLE IF NOT EXISTS people_data
AS SELECT * FROM delta.`/databricks-datasets/learning-spark-v2/people/people.delta`;
```

The above operations create a new managed table by using the schema that was inferred from the data. For managed tables, Databricks determines the location for the data.

To get the location, use the below SQL command:

```
DESCRIBE DETAIL people_data;
```

Upsert to a table

To merge a set of updates and insertions into an existing Delta table, user can use the MERGE INTO statement. For example, the following statement takes data from the source table(people_updates) and merges it into the target Delta table(people_data).

When there is a matching row in both tables, Delta Lake updates the data column using the given expression. When there is no matching row, Delta Lake adds a new row. This operation is known as an *upsert*.

```
MERGE INTO people_data
USING people_updates
ON people_data.id = people_updates.id
WHEN MATCHED THEN UPDATE SET *
WHEN NOT MATCHED THEN INSERT *;
```

If user specifies *, this update or insert all columns in the target table. This assumes that the source table has the same columns as those in the target table, otherwise the query will throw an error.

User must specify a value for every column in table while performing an INSERT operation.

Read a table

User can access data in Delta tables by the table name or the table path, as shown in the following examples:

```
df = spark.read.table(table_name)
display(df)
```

User can also read using the table path:

```
people_df = spark.read.load(table_path)
display(people_df)
```

Using SQL, User can read using the below code:

```
SELECT * FROM people_data
SELECT * FROM delta.`<path-to-table>`;
```

Write to a table

To atomically add new data to an existing Delta table, use **append** mode

```
df.write.mode("append").saveAsTable("people_data")
```

To overwrite any existing table:

```
df.write.mode("overwrite").saveAsTable("people_data")
```

Update a table

User can update data that matches a condition in a Delta table. For example, in a table named people_data, to change an abbreviation in the gender column from M or F to Male or Female, user can run the following:

Using SQL:

```
UPDATE people_data SET gender = 'Female' WHERE gender = 'F';
UPDATE people_data SET gender = 'Male' WHERE gender = 'M';
```

For a table located at a path at /tmp/delta/people-data, to change an abbreviation in the **gender** column from **M** or **F** to **Male** or **Female**, user can run the following:

```
UPDATE delta.`/tmp/delta/people-data` SET gender='Female' WHERE gender='F';
UPDATE delta.`/tmp/delta/people-data` SET gender = 'Male' WHERE gender='M';
```

Using Python:

```python
from delta.tables import *
from pyspark.sql.functions import *

deltaTable = DeltaTable.forPath(spark, '/tmp/delta/people-data')

deltaTable.update(
  condition = col('gender') == 'M',
  set = {'gender': lit('Male')}
)
```

Delete from a table

User can remove data that matches a condition from a Delta table. For instance, in a table named people-data, to delete all rows corresponding to people with a value in the birthDate column from before 1955, user can use the below code:

Using SQL:

```
DELETE FROM people10m WHERE birthDate < '1955-01-01'
```

In a table at path */tmp/delta/people-data*, to delete all rows corresponding to people with a value in the **birthDate** column from before 1955, user can use the below code:

```
DELETE FROM delta.`/tmp/delta/people-10m` WHERE birthDate < '1955-01-01'
```

Using Python:

```
from delta.tables import *
from pyspark.sql.functions import *
deltaTable = DeltaTable.forPath(spark, '/tmp/delta/people-data')
deltaTable.delete(col('birthDate') < '1960-01-01')
```

Display table history

To view the history of a table, use the DESCRIBE HISTORY statement, which provides information, including the table version, operation, user, and so on, for each write to a table.

```
DESCRIBE HISTORY people_data
```

Time travel

Delta Lake time travel allows to query an older snapshot of a Delta table. To query an older version of a table, specify a version or timestamp in a SELECT statement. For example, to query version 0 from the history above, use:

```
SELECT * FROM people_data VERSION AS OF 0
```

To query based on timestamp, use:

```
SELECT * FROM people_data TIMESTAMP AS OF '2021-02-25 00:37:58'
```

Using Python, the above objective can be achieved using:

```
df1 = spark.read.format('delta').option('timestampAsOf', '2021-02-25').table("people_data")

df=spark.read.format('delta').option('versionAsOf',0).table("people_data")
```

Optimize a table

Once user has performed multiple changes to a table, user might have a lot of small files. To improve the speed of read queries, user can use OPTIMIZE to collapse small files into larger ones:

```
OPTIMIZE people_data
```

Z-order by columns

To improve read performance further, user can co-locate related information in the same set of files by Z-Ordering. This co-locality reduces the amount of data that needs to be read. To Z-Order data, user should specify the columns to order on in the ZORDER BY clause. For example, to co-locate by gender, run:

```
OPTIMIZE people_data
```

ZORDER BY (gender)

Clean up snapshots with VACUUM

To clean up old snapshots. User can do this by running the VACUUM command:

VACUUM people_data

Delta Lake table history

Each operation that modifies a Delta Lake table creates a new table version. User can use history information to audit operations, rollback a table, or query a table at a specific point in time using time travel.

User can retrieve information including the operations, user, and timestamp for each write to a Delta table by running the `history` command. Table history retention is determined by the table setting *delta.logRetentionDuration*, which is 30 days by default.

Using the below SQL command, user can get the history of the table:

DESCRIBE HISTORY eventsTable

Delta Lake time travel

Delta Lake time travel supports querying previous table versions based on timestamp or table version. SQL command to retrieve the data based on timestamp or version is shown below:

```
SELECT * FROM people_data TIMESTAMP AS OF '2020-12-18T22:15:12.013Z'
SELECT * FROM delta.`/tmp/delta/people_data` VERSION AS OF 5
```

Using Python, user can achieve the same using the below command:

```
df1 = spark.read.option("timestampAsOf", "2020-12-18").table("people_data")
df2 = spark.read.option("versionAsOf", 5).load("/tmp/delta/people_data")
```

Delta Lake records table versions as JSON files within the *_delta_log* directory, which is stored alongside table data.

To query a previous table version, user must retain both the log and the data files for that version. The default retention value is 7 days. Data files are deleted when VACUUM runs against a table. To increase the data retention threshold for Delta tables, user must configure the following table properties:

- delta.logRetentionDuration = "interval <interval>". It controls how long the history for a table is kept. The default is "interval 30 days".

- delta.deletedFileRetentionDuration = "interval <interval>". It will retain the files for this interval duration. The default is "interval 7 days".

Restore a Delta table to an earlier state

User can restore a Delta table to its earlier state by using the RESTORE command. A Delta table internally maintains historic versions of the table that enable it to be restored to an earlier state. User can restore the table to earlier version or timestamp using the query:

```
RESTORE TABLE db.target_table TO VERSION AS OF <version>
RESTORE TABLE delta.`/data/target/` TO TIMESTAMP AS OF <timestamp>
```

Vacuum unused data files

User can remove data files no longer referenced by a Delta table that are older than the retention threshold by running the VACUUM command on the table. Running VACUUM regularly helps in reducing the cloud storage cost by deleting unused files. The syntax for running vacuum is:

```
VACUUM tablename
```

The above command will vacuum files which are not required by versions older than the default retention period.

```
VACUUM '/data/events' -- vacuum files in path-based table

VACUUM delta.`/data/events/` RETAIN 100 HOURS  -- vacuum files more than 100 hours old

VACUUM eventsTable DRY RUN   -- do dry run to get the list of files to be deleted
```

Databricks recommends regularly running VACUUM on all tables to reduce excess cloud data storage costs. The default retention threshold for vacuum is 7 days. It is recommended that user sets a retention interval to be at least 7 days, because old snapshots and uncommitted files can still be in use by concurrent readers or writers to the table.

Optimize Tables

Delta Lake on Azure Databricks can improve the speed of read queries from a table. One way to improve this speed is to coalesce small files into larger ones.

User can trigger compaction by running the OPTIMIZE command. User can achieve this for events table using:

```
--path-based table
OPTIMIZE delta.`/data/events`
OPTIMIZE events
```

Using Python:

```python
from delta.tables import *
deltaTable = DeltaTable.forPath(spark, "/data/events")
deltaTable.optimize().executeCompaction()
```

If User has a large amount of data and only wants to optimize a subset of it, user can specify an optional partition predicate using WHERE:

```sql
OPTIMIZE events WHERE date >= '2020-12-18'
```

Using Python:

```python
from delta.tables import *
deltaTable = DeltaTable.forName(spark, "events")
deltaTable.optimize().where("date='2020-12-18'").executeCompaction()
```

OPTIMIZE makes no data related changes to the table, so a read before and after an OPTIMIZE has the same results.

When user chooses to run OPTIMIZE, there is a trade-off between performance and cost. Running OPTIMIZE command incur a higher cost because of the increased resource usage. Running OPTIMIZE command is a CPU intensive operation doing large amounts of Parquet decoding and encoding so Databricks recommends Compute optimized instance types for cluster.

Z-order indexes

Z-ordering is a technique to co-locate related information in the same set of files. This co-locality is automatically used by Delta Lake on Azure Databricks data-skipping algorithms. This behaviour dramatically reduces the amount of data that Delta Lake on Azure Databricks needs to read. To Z-order data, user should specify the columns to order on in the ZORDER BY clause:

If user expects a column to be commonly used in query predicates and if that column has high cardinality (many distinct values), then use ZORDER BY.

```sql
OPTIMIZE events
ZORDER BY (eventType)
```

User can specify multiple columns for ZORDER BY as a comma-separated list. However, the effectiveness of the locality drops with each extra column.

Change Data Feed

Change data feed allows Databricks to track row-level changes between versions of a Delta table. When enabled on a Delta table, the runtime records *change events* for all the data written into the table. This includes the row data along with metadata indicating whether the specified row was inserted, deleted, or updated.

User can read the change events in batch queries using Spark SQL, Apache Spark DataFrames, and Structured Streaming.

Change data feed works in tandem with table history to provide change information so change data feed on cloned tables doesn't match that of the original table. This is because the cloned table has a separate history.

Use cases

Change data feed is not enabled by default. Some of the use cases that improves the performance are:

- *Silver and Gold tables*: Improve Delta Lake performance by processing only row-level changes to accelerate and simplify ETL and ELT operations.
- *Materialized views*: Create up-to-date, aggregated views of information for use in BI and analytics without having to reprocess the full underlying tables, instead updating only where changes have come through.

Enable change data feed

User must explicitly enable the change data feed option using one of the following methods:

- *New table*: Set the table property `delta.enableChangeDataFeed` = true in the CREATE TABLE command.

  CREATE TABLE student (id INT, name STRING, age INT) TBLPROPERTIES
  (delta.enableChangeDataFeed = true)

- *Existing table*: Set the table property `delta.enableChangeDataFeed` = true in the ALTER TABLE command.

  ALTER TABLE myDeltaTable SET TBLPROPERTIES(delta.enableChangeDataFeed = true)

- *All new tables*:

  set spark.databricks.delta.properties.defaults.enableChangeDataFeed = true;

Read changes in batch queries

To read the changes, user can provide either version or timestamp for the start and end. To read the changes from a particular start version to the latest version of the table, specify only the starting version or timestamp.

Using SQL:

```
-- capture changes from version 0 to 10
SELECT * FROM table_changes('tableName', 0, 10)


-- Capture changes between timestamps
SELECT * FROM table_changes('tableName', '2021-04-21 05:45:46', '2021-05-21 12:00:00')

-- providing only the startingVersion/timestamp. It will capture changes from this version to latest version
SELECT * FROM table_changes('tableName', 5)


-- path based tables
SELECT * FROM table_changes_by_path('\path', '2022-08-21 05:50:46')
```

Using Python:

```python
spark.read.format("delta") \
  .option("readChangeFeed", "true") \
  .option("startingVersion", 0) \
  .option("endingVersion", 10) \
  .table("myDeltaTable")


spark.read.format("delta") \
  .option("readChangeFeed", "true") \
  .option("startingTimestamp", '2021-04-21 05:45:46') \
  .option("endingTimestamp", '2021-05-21 12:00:00') \
  .table("myDeltaTable")


# providing only the startingVersion/timestamp
spark.read.format("delta") \
  .option("readChangeFeed", "true") \
  .option("startingVersion", 5) \
  .table("myDeltaTable")


# path based tables
spark.read.format("delta") \
  .option("readChangeFeed", "true") \
  .option("startingTimestamp", '2022-08-21 05:50:46') \
  .load("pathToMyDeltaTable")
```


Read changes in streaming queries

```python
# providing a starting version
```

```
spark.readStream.format("delta") \
  .option("readChangeFeed", "true") \
  .option("startingVersion", 5) \
  .table("myDeltaTable")


# providing a starting timestamp
spark.readStream.format("delta") \
  .option("readChangeFeed", "true") \
  .option("startingTimestamp", "2022-06-21 05:35:43") \
  .load("/pathToMyDeltaTable")


#Not providing a starting version/timestamp will result in the latest snapshot being fetched first
spark.readStream.format("delta") \
  .option("readChangeFeed", "true") \
  .table("myDeltaTable")
```

To get the change data while reading the table, set the option *readChangeFeed* to true.

The *startingVersion* or *startingTimestamp* are optional and if not provided the stream returns the latest snapshot of the table at the time of streaming as an **INSERT** and future changes as change data. When user reads from the change data feed for a table, the schema for the latest table version is used.

Table constraint

Databricks supports standard SQL constraint management clauses. All constraints on Databricks require Delta Lake. Databricks supports two types of constraint:

- *NOT NULL*: indicates that values in specific columns cannot be null.
  ```
  CREATE TABLE people_data (
    id INT NOT NULL,
    firstName STRING,
    middleName STRING NOT NULL,
    lastName STRING,
    gender STRING,
    birthDate TIMESTAMP,
    salary INT
  ) USING DELTA;
  ```

- *CHECK*: indicates that a specified boolean expression must be true for each input row. User can add constraint on the table.

  ```
  ALTER TABLE people_data ADD CONSTRAINT dateWithinRange CHECK (birthDate > '1900-01-01');
  ```

Upsert into a Delta Lake table using merge

User can upsert data from a source table, view, or DataFrame into a target Delta table by using the **MERGE** SQL operation. Delta Lake supports inserts, updates, and deletes in **MERGE**.

Suppose user has a source table named **source** or a source path that contains new data for a target table named **target** or a target path. Some of these new records may already be present in the target data. To merge the new data, user wants to update rows where the key is already present in target table and insert the new rows where no matching **key** is present. User can run the following query using SQL:

```
MERGE INTO target
USING source
ON source.key = target.key
WHEN MATCHED THEN
  UPDATE SET *
WHEN NOT MATCHED THEN
  INSERT *
WHEN NOT MATCHED BY SOURCE THEN
  DELETE
```

There are three conditions in above query:

- MATCHED: - The target table has some rows which are present in source table based on key. These rows on target table will be updated with source rows values.
- NOT MATCHED: The source table has some rows that do not exist in the target table based on key. These rows will be inserted in target table.
- NOT MATCHED BY SOURCE: The target table has some rows that do not exist in the source table. These rows will be deleted from the target tables. User needs to use this condition when user wants to synchronize the target table with the data from the source table.

The above code can be written in python like:

```
(targetDF
 .merge(sourceDF, "source.key = target.key")
 .whenMatchedUpdateAll()
 .whenNotMatchedInsertAll()
 .whenNotMatchedBySourceDelete()
 .execute()
)
```

In case User needs to update some fields then user can specify the fields values as well.

```
MERGE INTO people_data
USING people_data_updates
ON people_data.id = people_data_updates.id
WHEN MATCHED THEN
  UPDATE SET
    firstName = people_data_updates.firstName,
    middleName = people_data_updates.middleName,
    lastName = people_data_updates.lastName
WHEN NOT MATCHED
  THEN INSERT (
  id,
  firstName,
  middleName,
  lastName
 )
  VALUES (
  people_data_updates.id,
  people_data_updates.firstName,
  people_data_updates.middleName,
  people_data_updates.lastName
 )
```

Custom Metadata

User can enrich Delta Lake tables with custom metadata. User can use fields in the Delta Lake transaction log to add custom tags to a table or messages for an individual commit.

User can specify user-defined strings as metadata in commits by using the DataFrameWriter option *userMetadata*.

```
df.write.format("delta") \
  .mode("overwrite") \
  .option("userMetadata", "fixing-incorrect-data") \
  .save("/tmp/delta/people_data")
```

This user-defined metadata is readable through describe history command.

User can store its own metadata as a table property using TBLPROPERTIES in CREATE and ALTER.

```
ALTER TABLE people_data SET TBLPROPERTIES ('department' = 'accounting')
```

User can then display that metadata:

114

```
-- Show just the 'department' table property.
SHOW TBLPROPERTIES people_data ('department')
```

Generated columns

Delta Lake supports generated columns which are a special type of column whose values are automatically generated based on a user-specified function over other columns in the Delta table. The column value is automatically computed based on the user-defined function applied for the generated column.

```
CREATE TABLE people_data (
  id INT,
  firstName STRING,
  middleName STRING,
  birthDate TIMESTAMP,
  yearofBirth INT GENERATED ALWAYS AS (YEAR(birthDate))
)
PARTITIONED BY yearofBirth
```

User can define identity columns in delta lake table. Delta Lake identity columns are a type of generated column that assign unique values for each record inserted to a table. Identity columns only support the BIGINT type. User can optionally specify a starting value and a step size.

Tables cannot be partitioned by an identity column, and user cannot perform update operations on identity columns.

Declaring an identity column on a Delta table disables concurrent transactions. In use cases, only use identity columns where concurrent writes to the target table are not required.

Idempotent writes

Sometimes a job that writes data to a Delta table is restarted due to various reasons e.g., job encounters a failure. The failed job may or may not have written the data to Delta table before terminating. In the case where the data is written again, the restarted job writes the same data to the Delta table which results in duplicate data.

To address this, Delta tables support the following *DataFrameWriter* options to make the writes idempotent:

- *txnAppId:* A unique string that user can pass on each DataFrame write.
- *txnVersion:* A monotonically increasing number that acts as transaction version. This number needs to be unique for data that is being written to the Delta table(s). Any subsequent restarts of the same job need to have the same value for txnVersion.

The above combination of options needs to be unique for each new data that is being ingested into the Delta table and the *txnVersion* needs to be higher than the last data that was ingested into the Delta table.

```
app_id = # A unique string that is used as an application ID.
Version = # A monotonically increasing number that acts as transaction version.


dataFrame.write.option("txnVersion", version).option("txnAppId", app_id).save(...)
```

Delta Lake schema validation

Delta Lake automatically validates that the schema of the DataFrame being written is compatible with the schema of the table. Delta Lake uses the following rules to determine whether a write from a DataFrame to a table is compatible:

- All DataFrame columns must exist in the target table. If there are columns in the DataFrame not present in the table, an exception is raised. Columns present in the table but not in the DataFrame are set to null.
- DataFrame column data types must match the column data types in the target table.
- DataFrame columns name must be unique. Same column name (even if it is case sensitive) can't be in dataframe.

Merge automatically validates that the schema of the data generated by insert and update expressions are compatible with the schema of the table. It uses the following rules for compatibility:

- For update and insert actions, the specified target columns must exist in the target Delta table.
- For updateAll and insertAll actions, the source dataset must have all the columns of the target Delta table. The source dataset can have extra columns and they are ignored.

Selectively overwrite

Databricks leverages Delta Lake functionality to support for selective overwrite. User can selectively overwrite only the data that matches an arbitrary expression.

The following command replaces events in January in the target table with the data in dataframe df which satisfies the given condition.

```
df.write
  .mode("overwrite")
  .option("replaceWhere", "start_date >= '2020-01-01' AND end_date <= '2022-01-31'")
  .save("/tmp/delta/events")
```

Update Schema

Delta Lake lets user update the schema of a table. The following types of changes are supported:
- Adding new columns (at arbitrary positions)
- Reordering existing columns
- Renaming existing columns

Partitioning Tables

Most tables with less than 1 TB of data do not require partitions. Databricks recommends all partitions contain at least 1 GB of data. Tables with fewer, larger partitions tend to outperform tables with many smaller partitions.

Partitioning works well only for low or known cardinality fields (for example, date fields or physical locations), but not for fields with high cardinality such as timestamps.

Clone Delta Table

User can create a copy of an existing Delta Lake table on Databricks at a specific version using the *clone* command. Clones can be either deep or shallow.

Clone types

A *deep clone* is a clone that copies the source table data to the clone target in addition to the metadata of the existing table.

A *shallow clone* is a clone that does not copy the data to the clone target. The table metadata is copied. Shallow clones reference data files in the source directory of source table. The metadata that is cloned includes: schema, partitioning information, invariants, nullability.

In Databricks Runtime 13.1 and above, Unity Catalog managed tables have support for shallow clones.

- Any changes made to either deep or shallow clones affect only the clones themselves and not the source table.
- Deep clones are expensive to create than Shallow clones.
- Cloning a table is not the same as Create Table As Select or CTAS. A clone copies the metadata of the source table in addition to the data. Cloning also has simpler syntax. User doesn't need to specify partitioning, format, invariants, nullability and so on as they are taken from the source table.
- A cloned table has an independent history from its source table. Time travel queries on a cloned table do not work with the same inputs as they work on its source table.

To Create Deep Clone:

CREATE TABLE delta.`/data/target/` CLONE delta.`/data/source/` -- Creates a deep clone of /data/source at /data/target

CREATE OR REPLACE TABLE db.target_table CLONE db.source_table -- Replace the target

117

CREATE TABLE IF NOT EXISTS delta.`/data/target/` CLONE db.source_table -- No-op if the target table exists

To Create Shallow clone:

CREATE TABLE db.target_table SHALLOW CLONE delta.`/data/source`

User can clone a specific version as well:

CREATE TABLE db.target_table SHALLOW CLONE delta.`/data/source` VERSION AS OF version

CREATE TABLE db.target_table SHALLOW CLONE delta.`/data/source` TIMESTAMP AS OF timestamp_expression
-- timestamp can be like "2022-02-01" or like date_sub(current_date(), 1)

Using Python:

```
from delta.tables import *
deltaTable = DeltaTable.forPath(spark, pathToTable)     # path-based tables, or
deltaTable = DeltaTable.forName(spark, tableName)       # Hive metastore-based tables
deltaTable.clone(target, isShallow, replace) # clone the source at latest version
```

The following permissions are required for both deep and shallow clones:

- SELECT permission on the source table.
- If user is using CLONE to create a new table, CREATE permission on the database in which user is creating the table.
- If user is using CLONE to replace a table, user must have MODIFY permission on the table.

Any user that reads the deep clone must have read access to the clone's directory. To make changes to the clone, users must have write access to the clone's directory.

For Shallow clone, any user that reads the shallow clone needs permission to read the files in the original table. To make changes to the clone, users will need write access to the clone's directory.

Clone for data archiving

User can use deep clone to preserve the state of a table at a certain point in time for archival purposes. User can create deep clones to maintain an updated state of a source table for disaster recovery.

CREATE OR REPLACE TABLE delta.`/some/archive/path` CLONE my_prod_table

Clone on Unity Catalog

User can use shallow clone to create new Unity Catalog managed tables from existing Unity Catalog managed tables. Shallow clone support for Unity Catalog allows user to create tables with access control privileges independent from their parent tables without needing to copy underlying data files.

Create a shallow clone

The syntax to shallow clone unity catalog table is:

CREATE TABLE <catalog-name>.<schema-name>.<target-table-name> SHALLOW CLONE <catalog-name>.<schema-name>.<source-table-name>

To create a shallow clone on Unity Catalog, user must have sufficient privileges on both the source and target resources. The permissions required are:

Resource	Permissions required
Source table	SELECT
Source schema	USE SCHEMA
Source catalog	USE CATALOG
Target schema	USE SCHEMA, CREATE TABLE
Target catalog	USE CATALOG

Query or modify a shallow cloned table

To query a shallow clone on Unity Catalog, user must have sufficient privileges on the table and containing resources, as detailed in the following table:

Resource	Permissions required
Catalog	USE CATALOG
Schema	USE SCHEMA
Table	SELECT

Data governance

Data governance ensures that data brings value and supports the business strategy. Data governance encapsulates the policies and practices to securely manage the data assets within an organization. As the amount and complexity of data are growing, more and more organizations are looking at data governance to ensure the core business outcomes. Data governance provides the following outcomes:

- Consistent and high data quality.
- Reduced time to insight.
- Data democratization, that is enabling everybody in an organization to make data-driven decisions.
- Support for risk and compliance for industry regulations such as HIPAA, FedRAMP, GDPR, or CCPA.
- Cost optimization, for example by preventing users to start up large clusters and creating guardrails for using expensive GPU instances.

Data-driven companies typically build their data architectures for analytics on the Lakehouse. Data governance for a data lakehouse provides the following key capabilities:

- Unified catalog: A unified catalog stores all data, ML models, and analytics artifacts, in addition to metadata for each data object.
- Unified data access controls: A single and unified permissions model across all data assets and all clouds.
- Data isolation: Data isolation can be achieved at many levels like environment, storage location, data objects of increasing granularity without losing the ability to manage access and auditing centrally.
- Data auditing: Data access is centrally audited with alerts and monitoring capabilities to promote accountability.
- Data quality management: Robust data quality management with built-in quality controls, testing, monitoring, and enforcement to ensure accurate and useful data.
- Data lineage: Data lineage to get end-to-end visibility into how data flows in Lakehouse from source to consumption.
- Data discovery: Easy data discovery to enable data scientists, data analysts, and data engineers to quickly discover and reference relevant data.
- Data sharing: Data can be shared across clouds and platforms.

Azure Databricks provides centralized governance for data and AI with Unity Catalog and Delta Sharing.

Unity Catalog

Unity Catalog provides centralized access control, auditing, lineage, and data discovery capabilities across Azure Databricks workspaces.

Key features of Unity Catalog include:

- Unity Catalog offers a single place to administer data access policies that apply across all workspaces.
- Unity Catalog's security model allows administrators to grant permissions in their existing data lake at the level of catalogs, databases (also called schemas), tables, and views.
- Unity Catalog automatically captures user-level audit logs that record access to data.
- Unity Catalog captures lineage data that tracks how data assets are created and used across all languages.
- Unity Catalog lets user tag and document data assets and provides a search interface to help data consumers find data.
- Unity Catalog lets user easily access and query account's operational data, including audit logs, billable usage, and lineage.

Unity Catalog object model

In Unity Catalog, the hierarchy of primary data objects flows from metastore to table or volume:

- Metastore: The top-level container for metadata. Each metastore exposes a three-level namespace (catalog.schema.table) that organizes data.
- Catalog: The first layer of the object hierarchy, used to organize data assets.
- Schema: Also known as databases, schemas are the second layer of the object hierarchy and contain tables and views.
- Volume: Volumes sit alongside tables and views at the lowest level of the object hierarchy and provide governance for non-tabular data.
- Table: At the lowest level in the object hierarchy are tables and views.

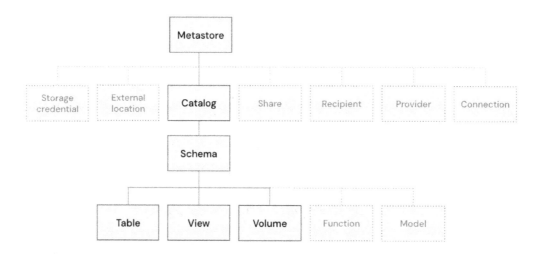

Metastores

A metastore is the top-level container of objects in Unity Catalog. It stores metadata about data assets (tables and views) and the permissions that govern access to them. Metastore should be created and assigned to Azure Databricks workspaces in the same region. For a workspace to use Unity Catalog, it must have a Unity Catalog metastore attached.

This metastore is distinct from the Hive metastore. If workspace includes a legacy Hive metastore, the data in that metastore will still be available alongside data defined in Unity Catalog, in a catalog named *hive_metastore*. hive_metastore catalog is not managed by Unity Catalog and does not benefit from the same feature set as catalogs defined in Unity Catalog.

Each metastore is configured with a managed storage location in cloud storage e.g. an Azure Data Lake Storage Gen2 container in Azure account.

Managed storage

When an account admin creates a metastore, account admin must associate a storage location in cloud storage e.g. an Azure Data Lake Storage Gen2 container in Azure account to use as *managed storage*.

Managed tables and managed volumes store data and metadata files in managed storage. Managed storage cannot overlap with external tables, external volumes, or other managed storage.

Catalog

A catalog is the first layer of Unity Catalog's three-level namespace. It's used to organize data assets. Users can see all catalogs on which they have been assigned the USE CATALOG data permission.

Schemas

A schema (also called a database) is the second layer of Unity Catalog's three-level namespace. A schema organizes tables and views. Users can see all schemas on which they have been assigned the USE SCHEMA permission, along with the USE CATALOG permission on the schema's parent catalog. To access or list a table or view in a schema, users must also have SELECT permission on the table or view.

Tables

A table resides in the third layer of Unity Catalog's three-level namespace. It contains rows of data. To create a table, users must have CREATE and USE SCHEMA permissions on the schema, and they must have the USE CATALOG permission on its parent catalog. To query a table, users must have the SELECT permission on the table, the USE SCHEMA permission on its parent schema, and the USE CATALOG permission on its parent catalog. A table can be managed or external.

Managed Table:

Managed tables are the default way to create tables in Unity Catalog. Unity Catalog manages the lifecycle and file layout for these tables.

By default, managed tables are stored in the root storage location that user configures while creating a metastore. User can optionally specify managed table storage locations at the catalog or schema levels, overriding the root storage location. Managed tables always use the Delta table format.

When a managed table is dropped, its underlying data is deleted from our cloud tenant within 30 days.

External tables

External tables are tables whose data lifecycle and file layout are not managed by Unity Catalog. When user drops an external table, Unity Catalog does not delete the underlying data. User can manage privileges on external tables and use them in queries in the same way as managed tables.

External tables can use the following file formats:
- DELTA
- CSV
- JSON
- AVRO
- PARQUET
- ORC
- TEXT

Views

A view is a read-only object created from one or more tables and views in a metastore. It resides in the third layer of Unity Catalog's three-level namespace. A view can be created from tables and other views in multiple schemas and catalogs.

Identity management for Unity Catalog

Unity Catalog uses the identities in the Databricks account to resolve users, service principals, and groups, and to enforce permissions.

Unity Catalog users, service principals, and groups must also be added to workspaces to access Unity Catalog data.

Admin roles for Unity Catalog

The following admin roles are required for managing Unity Catalog:
- *Account admins* can manage identities, cloud resources and the creation of workspaces and Unity Catalog metastores. Account admins can enable workspaces for Unity Catalog. They can grant both workspace and metastore admin permissions.
- *Metastore admins* can manage privileges and ownership for all securable objects within a metastore, such as who can create catalog or query a table. The account admin who

creates the Unity Catalog metastore becomes the initial metastore admin. The metastore admin can also choose to delegate this role to another user or group.

- *Workspace admins* can add users to an Databricks workspace, assign them the workspace admin role, and manage access to objects and functionality in the workspace, such as the ability to create clusters and change job ownership.

Data permissions in Unity Catalog

In Unity Catalog, data is secure by default. Initially, users have no access to data in a metastore. Access can be granted by either a metastore admin, the owner of an object, or the owner of the catalog or schema that contains the object.

Cluster access modes for Unity Catalog

To access data in Unity Catalog, clusters must be configured with the correct *access mode*. If a cluster is not configured with one of the Unity-Catalog-capable access modes (that is, shared or assigned), the cluster can't access data in Unity Catalog.

Data lineage for Unity Catalog

User can use Unity Catalog to capture runtime data lineage across queries. Lineage is captured down to the column level, and includes notebooks, workflows and dashboards related to the query.

Unity Catalog metastore

A metastore is the top-level container of objects in Unity Catalog. It stores metadata about data assets (tables and views) and the permissions that govern access to them. User must create one metastore for each region in which the organization operates. To create a metastore:

- User must be an Databricks account admin.
- The workspaces that user attach to the metastore must be on the Databricks Premium plan.
- User must have permission to create:
    - A storage account to use e.g. Azure Data Lake Storage Gen2.
    - Be a Contributor or Owner of a resource group in any subscription in the tenant.
- Create a storage container where the metastore's managed table data will be stored. This storage container must be in an Azure Data Lake Storage Gen2 account in the same region as the workspaces user want to use to access the data.
- Create an identity that Databricks uses to give access to that storage container. User can use either an Azure managed identity or a service principal as the identity that gives access to the metastore's storage container.

    Unlike service principals, managed identities do not require to maintain credentials or rotate secrets, and they let user connect to an Azure Data Lake Storage Gen2 account that is protected by a storage firewall.
- Provide Databricks with the storage container path and identity.

Create a metastore

- Create an Azure Databricks access connector and assign it permissions to the storage container where user wants the metastore's managed tables to be stored.

  An Azure Databricks access connector is a first-party Azure resource that lets user connect a system-assigned managed identity to an Azure Databricks account. Make a note of the access connector's resource ID.

- Log in to the Azure Databricks account console.
- Click Data
- Click *Create Metastore*.
- Enter values for the following field
  - *Name* for the metastore.
  - *Region* where the metastore will be deployed. This must be the same region as the workspaces user wants to use to access the data. Make sure that it matches the region of the access connector and storage container that user created earlier.
  - *ADLS Gen 2 path*: Enter the path to the storage container that user will use as the default root storage for managed table data.
  - *Access Connector ID*: Enter the Azure Databricks access connector's resource ID.
- Click *Create*.
- When prompted, select workspaces to link to the metastore.

Enable a workspace for Unity Catalog

To enable an Azure Databricks workspace for Unity Catalog, user should assign the workspace to a Unity Catalog metastore. A metastore is the top-level container for data in Unity Catalog. Each metastore exposes a 3-level namespace (catalog.schema.table) by which data can be organized.

User can share a single metastore across multiple Databricks workspaces in an account. Each linked workspace has the same view of the data in the metastore, and user can manage data access control across workspaces. User can create one metastore per region and attach it to any number of workspaces in that region.

Before user can enable workspace for Unity Catalog, user must have a Unity Catalog metastore configured for Databricks account.

To enable an existing workspace:
- As an account admin, log in to the account console
- Click data
- Click the metastore name.
- Click the Workspaces tab.
- Click Assign to workspaces.
- Select one or more workspaces.

- Click Assign
- On the confirmation dialog, click Enable.

To enable Unity Catalog when user creates a workspace:

- As an account admin, log in to the account console.
- Click Workspaces
- Click the Enable Unity Catalog toggle.
- Select the Metastore.
- On the confirmation dialog, click Enable.
- Complete the workspace creation configuration and click Save.

When the assignment is complete, the workspace appears in the metastore's Workspaces tab, and the metastore appears on the workspace's Configuration tab.

Create clusters & SQL warehouses with Unity Catalog access

SQL warehouses are used to run Databricks SQL workloads, such as queries, dashboards, and visualizations. SQL warehouses allow user to access Unity Catalog data and run Unity Catalog-specific commands by default, as long as workspace is attached to a Unity Catalog metastore.

Clusters are used to run workloads using notebooks or automated jobs. To create a cluster that can access Unity Catalog, the cluster must be attached to a Unity Catalog metastore and must use a Unity-Catalog-capable access mode (shared or single user).

User can work with data in Unity Catalog using either of SQL warehouses for SQL Editor or clusters for notebooks.

To create a cluster that can access Unity Catalog, the workspace must be attached to a Unity Catalog metastore. Unity Catalog requires clusters that run Databricks Runtime 11.3 LTS or above.

Create and manage Catalogs

To create catalog, following requirements should be met:

- User must be an Databricks metastore admin or have been granted the CREATE CATALOG privilege on the metastore
- Databricks account must be on the Premium plan.
- User must have a Unity Catalog metastore linked to the workspace where user can perform the catalog creation.
- The compute resource that user use to run the notebook or Databricks SQL to create the catalog must be using a Unity Catalog compliant access mode.

To create a catalog, user can use Data Explorer or a SQL command. The steps are:

Data Explorer:
- Log in to a workspace that is linked to the metastore.

- Click Data icon.
- Click the *Create Catalog* button.
- Optionally specify the location where data for managed tables in the catalog will be stored. Specify a location here only if user does not want managed tables in this catalog to be stored in the default root storage location (configured for the metastore).
  The path that user specifies must be defined in an external location configuration, and user must have the **CREATE MANAGED STORAGE** privilege on that external location. User can also use a subpath of that path.
- Click Create.

By default, the catalog is shared with all workspaces attached to the current metastore. If the catalog will contain data that should be restricted to specific workspaces, go to the Workspaces tab and add those workspaces. Assign permissions for catalog.

Using SQL

The SQL syntax for creating catalog is:

```
CREATE CATALOG [ IF NOT EXISTS ] <catalog-name>
  [ MANAGED LOCATION '<location-path>' ]
  [ COMMENT <comment> ];
```

- <catalog-name>: A name for the catalog.
- <location-path>: Optional. Provide a storage location path if user wants managed tables in this catalog to be stored in a location that is different than the default that was configured for the metastore.
- <comment>: Optional description or other comment.

For example, to create a catalog named testcatalog

```
CREATE CATALOG IF NOT EXISTS testcatalog;
```

Assign the required privileges to the catalog.

Using Python:

To create the catalog using python:

```
spark.sql("CREATE CATALOG IF NOT EXISTS testcatalog")
```

The default is to share the catalog with all workspaces attached to the current metastore. User can optionally assign a catalog to specific workspaces. If user uses workspaces to isolate user data access, user may want to limit catalog access to specific workspaces in his account. Typical use cases for binding a catalog to specific workspaces include:

- Ensuring that users can only access production data from a production workspace environment.
- Ensuring that users can only process sensitive data from a dedicated workspace.

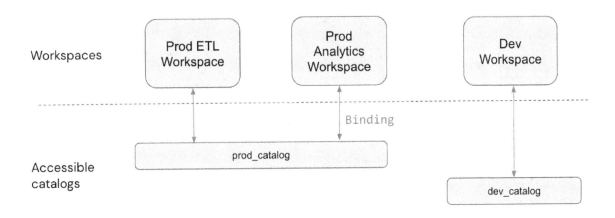

In this diagram, `prod_catalog` is bound to two production workspaces. Suppose a user has been granted access to a table in `prod_catalog` called `my_table`(using `GRANT SELECT ON my_table TO <user>`). The user can access `my_table` only from the Prod ETL and Prod Analytics workspaces. If the user tries to access `my_table` in the Dev workspace, user will receive an error message.

Only Metastore admin or catalog owner can assign a catalog to specific workspaces. To assign a catalog to specific workspaces:

- Log in to a workspace that is linked to the metastore
- Click Data
- In the Data pane, on the left, click the catalog name. Data Explorer pane will show the Catalogs list. Select the catalog from the list.
- On the *Workspaces* tab, clear the *All workspaces have access* checkbox.
- Click *Assign to workspaces* and enter or find the workspace user wants to assign.

To revoke access, go to the *Workspaces* tab, select the workspace, and click *Revoke*.

To view information about a catalog, user can use Data Explorer or a SQL command.

Data explorer:
- Log in to a workspace that is linked to the metastore.
- Click Data
- In the *Data* pane, find the catalog and click its name. Some details are listed at the top of the page. Others can be viewed on the *Schemas, Details, Permissions and Workspaces* tabs.

SQL

User can run the SQL command in a notebook or Databricks SQL editor. The following command returns the metadata of an existing catalog. The metadata information includes catalog name, comment, and owner.

DESCRIBE CATALOG <catalog-name>;

Use CATALOG EXTENDED to get full details.

To drop catalog:

DROP CATALOG [IF EXISTS] <catalog-name> [RESTRICT | CASCADE]

If user uses DROP CATALOG without the CASCADE option, user must delete all schemas in the catalog except *information_schema* before user can delete the catalog. This includes the auto-created default schema. Use CASCADE option to delete catalog with all its schema.

For example, to delete a catalog named testcatalog and its schemas:

DROP CATALOG testcatalog CASCADE

Python code to delete a catalog named **testcatalog** and its schemas:

spark.sql("DROP CATALOG testcatalog CASCADE")

Create and manage schemas (databases)

A schema contains tables, views, and functions. Schema is created inside catalog.

Requirements:

- User must have the USE CATALOG and CREATE SCHEMA data permissions on the schema's parent catalog. All users have the USE CATALOG permission on the main catalog by default.
- Databricks account must be on the Premium plan.
- Unity Catalog metastore must be linked to the workspace where user wants to create Schema.
- The compute resource that user uses to run the notebook or Databricks SQL to create the catalog must be using a Unity Catalog compliant access mode.

Create a schema

To create a schema (database), user can use Data Explorer or SQL commands.

- Log in to a workspace that is linked to the metastore.
- Click Data
- In the Data pane on the left, click the catalog where user wants to create the schema in.
- In the detail pane, click Create database.
- Give the schema a name
- Optionally, specify the location where data for managed tables in the schema will be stored. Specify a location here only if user does not want managed tables in this schema to be stored in the default root storage location configured for the metastore.
- Click Create
- Click Save

SQL

Run the following SQL commands in a notebook or Databricks SQL editor. Items in brackets are optional.

```
USE CATALOG <catalog>;
CREATE { DATABASE | SCHEMA } [ IF NOT EXISTS ] <schema-name>
  [ MANAGED LOCATION '<location-path>' ]
  [ COMMENT <comment> ]
  [ WITH DBPROPERTIES ( <property-key = property_value [ , ... ]> ) ];
```

User can optionally omit the USE CATALOG statement and replace <schema-name> with <catalog-name>.<schema-name>.

Python

The code in python to create schema will be like:

```
spark.sql("USE CATALOG <catalog>")

spark.sql("CREATE { DATABASE | SCHEMA } [ IF NOT EXISTS ] <schema-name> " \
  "[ MANAGED LOCATION '<location-path>' ] " \
  "[ COMMENT <comment> ] " \
  "[ WITH DBPROPERTIES ( <property-key = property_value [ , ... ]> ) ]")
```

- <catalog-name>: The name of the parent catalog for the schema.
- <schema-name>: A name for the schema.
- <location-path>: Optional. Provide a storage location path if user wants managed tables in this schema to be stored in a location that is different than the catalog's or metastore's root storage location.
- <comment>: An optional comment.
- <property-key> = <property-value> [, ...]: The Spark SQL properties and values to set for the schema.

To drop the schema:

SQL:
DROP SCHEMA [IF EXISTS] <schema-name> [RESTRICT | CASCADE]

If user uses DROP SCHEMA without the CASCADE option, user must delete all tables in the schema before user can delete it.

For example, to delete a schema named testSchema and its tables:

DROP SCHEMA testSchema CASCADE

To drop schema using python,

spark.sql("DROP SCHEMA testSchema CASCADE")

Create Tables
Unity Catalog has two types of tables, *managed* and *external* tables.

Managed tables
Managed tables are the default way to create tables in Unity Catalog. Unity Catalog manages the lifecycle and file layout for these tables.

By default, managed tables are stored in the root storage location that user configures when user creates a metastore. User can optionally specify managed table storage locations at the catalog or schema levels, overriding the root storage location. Managed tables always use the Delta table format.

When a managed table is dropped, its underlying data is deleted from user's cloud tenant within 30 days.

To create a managed table, run the following SQL command.

CREATE TABLE <catalog-name>.<schema-name>.<table-name>
(
 <column-specification>
);

- <catalog-name>: The name of the catalog. This cannot be the hive_metastore catalog that is created automatically for the Hive metastore associated with the Azure Databricks workspace.

132

- <schema-name>: The name of the schema.
- <table-name>: A name for the table.
- <column-specification>: The name and data type for each column.

The python command will be:

```
spark.sql("CREATE TABLE <catalog-name>.<schema-name>.<table-name> "
 "("
 " <column-specification>"
 ")")
```

The below example creates a table of name Student in "main" catalog and default schema.

Using SQL:
```
CREATE TABLE main.default.Student
(
  StudentID INT,
  FirstName INT,
  LastName INT
);

INSERT INTO main.default.Student VALUES
  (10, 'Amit', 'Kumar'),
  (20, 'John', 'mathew');
```

To drop a table:

```
DROP TABLE IF EXISTS catalog_name.schema_name.table_name;
```

External tables

External tables are tables whose data is stored outside of the managed storage location specified for the metastore, catalog, or schema. Use external tables only when user requires direct access to the data outside of Azure Databricks clusters or Databricks SQL warehouses.

When user runs **DROP TABLE** on an external table, Unity Catalog does not delete the underlying data. To create an external table with SQL, specify a **LOCATION** path in the **CREATE TABLE** statement. External tables can use the following file formats:

- DELTA
- CSV
- JSON
- AVRO

133

- PARQUET
- ORC
- TEXT

To create external table, user must have the following permissions:

- *CREATE EXTERNAL TABLE* on the external location that references the cloud storage path user specifies.
- *CREATE TABLE* on the parent schema.
- *USE SCHEMA* on the parent schema.
- *USE CATALOG* on the parent catalog.

The following command creates an external table. It can be run on notebook or the SQL query editor.

```
CREATE TABLE <catalog>.<schema>.<table-name>
(
  <column-specification>
)
LOCATION 'abfss://<bucket-path>/<table-directory>';
```

- <catalog>: The name of the catalog that will contain the table.
- <schema>: The name of the schema that will contain the table.
- <table-name>: A name for the table.
- <column-specification>: The name and data type for each column.
- <bucket-path>: The path on cloud tenant where the table will be created.
- <table-directory>: A directory where the table will be created. Use a unique directory for each table.

Once a table is created in a path, users can no longer directly access the files in that path from Databricks even if they have been given privileges on an external location or storage credential to do so.

The python code for creating table will be like:

```
spark.sql("CREATE TABLE <catalog>.<schema>.<table-name> "
 "("
 " <column-specification>"
 ") "
 "LOCATION 'abfss://<bucket-path>/<table-directory>'")
```

Create a table from the files

To create a new managed table and populate it with data in cloud storage, use the following example:

```
CREATE TABLE <catalog>.<schema>.<table-name>
(
 <column-specification>
)
SELECT * from <format>.`abfss://<path-to-files>`;
```

Using python:

```
spark.sql("CREATE TABLE <catalog>.<schema>.<table-name> "
 "( "
 " <column-specification> "
 ") "
 "SELECT * from <format>.`abfss://<path-to-files>`")
```

To create an external table and populate it with data in user's cloud storage, add a LOCATION clause:

```
CREATE TABLE <catalog>.<schema>.<table-name>
(
   <column-specification>
)
USING <format>
LOCATION 'abfss://<table-location>'
SELECT * from <format>.`abfss://<path-to-files>`;
```

Using python:

```
spark.sql("CREATE TABLE <catalog>.<schema>.<table-name> "
 "( "
 " <column-specification> "
 ") "
 "USING <format> "
 "LOCATION 'abfss://<table-location>' "
 "SELECT * from <format>.`abfss://<path-to-files>`")
```

Insert records from a path into an existing table

To insert records from a bucket path into an existing table, use the COPY INTO command.

```
COPY INTO <catalog>.<schema>.<table>
FROM (
 SELECT *
 FROM 'abfss://<path-to-files>'
```

```
)
FILEFORMAT = <format>;
```

- <catalog>: The name of the table's parent catalog.
- <schema>: The name of the table's parent schema.
- <path-to-files>: The bucket path that contains the data files.
- <format>: The format of the files, for example delta.
- <table-location>: The bucket path where the table will be created.

User must have the following permissions:
- USE CATALOG on the parent catalog and USE SCHEMA on the schema.
- MODIFY on the table.
- READ FILES on the external location associated with the bucket path where the files are located, or directly on the storage credential if user is not using an external location.
- To insert records into an external table, user needs CREATE EXTERNAL TABLE on the bucket path where the table is located.

To insert into an external table, add a LOCATION clause:

```
COPY INTO <catalog>.<schema>.<table>
LOCATION 'abfss://<table-location>'
FROM (
  SELECT *
  FROM 'abfss://<path-to-files>'
)
FILEFORMAT = <format>;
```

Create views

A view is a read-only object composed from one or more tables and views in a metastore. It resides in the third layer of Unity Catalog's three-level namespace. A view can be created from tables and other views in multiple schemas and catalogs.

Dynamic views can be used to provide row and column-level access control, in addition to data masking.

The owner of a view must have the ability to read the tables and views referenced in the view. A reader of a view does not need the ability to read the tables and views referenced in the view, unless they are using a cluster with Single User access mode. To read from a view from a cluster with **Single User** access mode, user must have **SELECT** on all referenced tables and views.

Create a view

To create a view, run the following SQL command. Items in brackets are optional.

136

```
CREATE VIEW <catalog-name>.<schema-name>.<view-name> AS
SELECT <query>;
```

The python code for the view creation:

```
spark.sql("CREATE VIEW <catalog-name>.<schema-name>.<view-name> AS SELECT <query>")
```

SQL Example:

```
CREATE VIEW main.default.StudentView  AS
SELECT
 StudentID,
 FirstName,
 LastName,
FROM main.default.Student;
```

Drop a view

User must be the view's owner to drop a view. To drop a view, run the following SQL command:

```
DROP VIEW IF EXISTS catalog_name.schema_name.view_name;
```

Manage external locations and storage credentials

External locations and storage credentials allow Unity Catalog to read and write data on user's cloud tenant on behalf of users. These external locations and storage credentials are used for:

- Creating, reading from, and writing to external tables.
- Overriding the metastore's default managed table storage location at the catalog or schema level.
- Creating a managed or external table from files stored on user's cloud tenant.
- Inserting records into tables from files stored on user's cloud tenant.
- Directly exploring data files stored on user's cloud tenant.

Storage credentials

A storage credential represents an authentication and authorization mechanism for accessing data stored on user's cloud tenant, using either an Azure managed identity (strongly recommended) or a service principal.

Each storage credential is subject to Unity Catalog access-control policies that control which users and groups can access the credential. If a user does not have access to a storage credential in Unity Catalog, the request fails and Unity Catalog does not attempt to authenticate to cloud tenant on the user's behalf. User can mark a storage credential as [read-only] to prevent users from writing to external locations that use the storage credential.

137

An external location is an object that combines a cloud storage path with a storage credential that authorizes access to the cloud storage path. Each storage location is subject to Unity Catalog access-control policies that control which users and groups can access the credential. If a user does not have access to a storage location in Unity Catalog, the request fails and Unity Catalog does not attempt to authenticate to cloud tenant on the user's behalf.

User can mark an external location as [read-only] to prevent users from writing to that location, which means that users cannot create tables or volumes (whether external or managed) in that location.

External locations can be used not just to define storage locations for external tables and volumes, but also for managed tables and volumes. They can be used to define storage locations for managed tables and volumes at the catalog and schema levels, overriding the metastore root storage location.

Databricks recommends using external locations rather than using storage credentials directly.

- To create storage credentials, user must be an Azure Databricks account admin. The account admin who creates the storage credential can delegate ownership to another user or group to manage permissions on it.
- To create external locations, user must be a metastore admin or a user with the CREATE EXTERNAL LOCATION privilege.
- External locations must use Azure Data Lake Storage Gen2 storage accounts that have a hierarchical namespace.

Create a storage credential

User can use either an Azure managed identity or a service principal as the identity that authorizes access to our storage container. Managed identities are strongly recommended. They have the benefit of allowing Unity Catalog to access storage accounts protected by network rules, which isn't possible using service principals. Managed identities remove the need to manage and rotate secrets.

To create a storage credential using a managed identity:

- Create an Azure Databricks access connector and assign it permissions to the storage container that user would like to access. An Azure Databricks access connector lets us connect managed identities to an Azure Databricks account. Make a note of the access connector's resource ID.
- Log in to Unity Catalog-enabled Azure Databricks workspace as a user who has the account admin role on the Azure Databricks account.
- Click Data
- At the bottom of the screen, click *Storage Credentials*.
- Click *+Add* > *Add a storage credential*.

- On the *Create a new storage credential* dialog, select *Managed identity (recommended)*.
- Enter a name for the credential, and enter the access connector's resource ID.
- If user wants other users to have read-only access to the external locations that use this storage credential, select **Read only.** It is optional.
- Click Save.

To view the list of all storage credentials and to view a storage credential in a metastore, user can use Data Explorer or a SQL command.

Using Data explorer:

- Log in to a workspace that is linked to the metastore.
- Click Data.
- At the bottom of the screen, click Storage Credentials. This will display list of storage credentials.
- Click the name of a storage credential to see its properties.

Using SQL:

Run the following command in a notebook or the Databricks SQL editor to see all storage credentials.

SHOW STORAGE CREDENTIALS;

To see the properties of a given storage credential:

DESCRIBE STORAGE CREDENTIAL <credential-name>;

Using Python:

Run the following command in a notebook.

display(spark.sql("SHOW STORAGE CREDENTIALS"))

To see the properties of a given storage credential:

display(spark.sql("DESCRIBE STORAGE CREDENTIAL <credential-name>"))

Manage permissions for a storage credential

User can grant permissions directly on the storage credential, but Databricks strongly recommends that user references it in an external location and grant permissions to that instead. An external location combines a storage credential with a specific path and authorizes access only to that path and its contents.

User can grant and revoke the following permissions on a storage credential:

- CREATE TABLE

139

- READ FILES
- WRITE FILES

To show grants on a storage credential, use a command like the following:

SHOW GRANTS [<principal>] ON STORAGE CREDENTIAL <storage-credential-name>;

- <principal>: The email address of the account-level user or the name of the account level group to whom to grant the permission.
- <storage-credential-name>: The name of a storage credential.

Using Python:

display(spark.sql("SHOW GRANTS [<principal>] ON STORAGE CREDENTIAL <storage-credential-name>"))

To grant permission to a principle to create an external table using a storage credential directly:

GRANT CREATE EXTERNAL TABLE ON STORAGE CREDENTIAL <storage-credential-name> TO <principal>;

Using Python:

spark.sql("GRANT CREATE EXTERNAL TABLE ON STORAGE CREDENTIAL <storage-credential-name> TO <principal>")

To grant permission to select from an external table using a storage credential directly:

GRANT READ FILES ON STORAGE CREDENTIAL <storage-credential-name> TO <principal>;

Using Python

spark.sql("GRANT READ FILES ON STORAGE CREDENTIAL <storage-credential-name> TO <principal>")

Change the owner of a storage credential:
A storage credential's creator is its initial owner. To change the owner to a different account-level user or group, do the following:

Using SQL:
ALTER STORAGE CREDENTIAL <credential-name> OWNER TO <principal>;

Using Python:

spark.sql("ALTER STORAGE CREDENTIAL <credential-name> OWNER TO <principal>")

Delete a storage credential

Using SQL:

```
DROP STORAGE CREDENTIAL IF EXISTS <credential-name>;
```

Using Python:

```
spark.sql("DROP STORAGE CREDENTIAL IF EXISTS <credential-name>")
```

Manage external locations

User can create an external location using Data Explorer, the Databricks CLI, SQL commands in a notebook or Databricks SQL query, or Terraform.

Run the following SQL command in a notebook or the Databricks SQL editor.

```
CREATE EXTERNAL LOCATION <location-name>
 URL 'abfss://<container-name>@<storage-account>.dfs.core.windows.net/<path>'
 WITH ([STORAGE] CREDENTIAL <storage-credential-name>);
```

- <location-name>: A name for the external location.
- <bucket-path>: The path in cloud tenant that this external location grants access to.
- <storage-credential-name>: The name of the storage credential that contains details about a service principal that is authorized to read to and write from the storage container path.

External locations only support Azure Data Lake Storage Gen2 storage.

Describe an external location:

To see the properties of an external location, user can use Data Explorer or a SQL command. Run the following command in a notebook or the Databricks SQL editor. Replace <location-name> with the name of the location.

```
DESCRIBE EXTERNAL LOCATION <location-name>;
```

Using Python:

```
display(spark.sql("DESCRIBE EXTERNAL LOCATION <location-name>"))
```

Rename an external location:

```
ALTER EXTERNAL LOCATION <location-name> RENAME TO <new-location-name>;
```

Change external location URI:

```
ALTER EXTERNAL LOCATION location_name SET URL '<url>' [FORCE];
```

Change the storage credential of an external location:

ALTER EXTERNAL LOCATION <location-name> SET STORAGE CREDENTIAL <credential-name>

Manage permissions for an external location

User can grant and revoke the following permissions on an external location using Data Explorer, the Databricks CLI, SQL commands in a notebook or Databricks SQL query, or Terraform.

- CREATE TABLE
- READ FILES
- WRITE FILES

To show grants on an external location:

Using SQL:

SHOW GRANTS [<principal>] ON EXTERNAL LOCATION <location-name>;
- <location-name>: The name of the external location that authorizes reading from and writing to the storage container path in your cloud tenant.
- <principal>: The email address of an account-level user or the name of an account-level group.

Using Python:

display(spark.sql("SHOW GRANTS [<principal>] ON EXTERNAL LOCATION <location-name>"))

To grant permission to use an external location to create a table:

GRANT CREATE EXTERNAL TABLE ON EXTERNAL LOCATION <location-name> TO <principal>;

To grant permission to read files from an external location:

GRANT READ FILES ON EXTERNAL LOCATION <location-name> TO <principal>;

Change the owner of an external location:

An external location's creator is its initial owner. To change the owner to a different account-level user or group, run the following command in a notebook or the Databricks SQL editor

ALTER EXTERNAL LOCATION <location-name> OWNER TO <principal>

Delete an external location:

To delete (drop) an external location user must be its owner. To delete an external location, use the following command:

```
DROP EXTERNAL LOCATION IF EXISTS <location-name>;
```

Mark an external location or storage credential as read-only.

If user wants users to have read-only access to an external location, user can use Data Explorer to mark the external location as read-only.

If user wants users to have read-only access to all external locations that are referenced by a specific storage credential, user can use Data Explorer to mark that storage credential as read-only.

Making storage credentials and external locations read-only:
- Prevents users from writing to files in those external locations, regardless of any write permissions granted by the Azure managed identity and regardless of the Unity Catalog permissions granted on that external location.
- Prevents users from creating tables or volumes (whether external or managed) in those external locations.

To mark storage credentials and external locations as read-only:
- In Data Explorer, find the storage credential or external location, click the ⋮ kebab menu (also known as the three-dot menu) on the object row, and select *Edit*.
- On the edit dialog, select the *Read only* option.

Query data

To query data in a table or view, the user must have the USE CATALOG permission on the parent catalog, the USE SCHEMA permission on the parent schema, and the SELECT permission on the table or view.

To read from a view on a cluster that uses single-user access mode, the user must have **SELECT** on all referenced tables and views.

Three-level namespace notation

In Unity Catalog, a table or view is contained within a parent catalog and schema. User can refer to a table or view using two different styles of notation. User can use USE CATALOG and USE statements to specify the catalog and schema:

Using SQL:

```
USE CATALOG <catalog-name>;
USE SCHEMA <schema-name>;
SELECT * from <table-name>;
```

As an alternative, user can use three-level namespace notation:

```
SELECT * from <catalog-name>.<schema-name>.<table-name>;
```

Using Python:

```
spark.sql("USE CATALOG <catalog-name>")
spark.sql("USE SCHEMA <schema-name>")

display(spark.table("<table-name>"))
```

Explore tables and views in Databricks SQL

User can explore tables and views without the need to run a cluster by using Data Explorer.
- To open Data Explorer, click Data in the sidebar.
- In Data Explorer, select the catalog and schema to view its tables and views.

For objects in the Hive Metastore, user must be running a SQL warehouse to use Data Explorer.

To select from a table or view using a notebook:

- In the sidebar, click New > Notebook.
- Attach the notebook to a SQL warehouse or cluster that uses an access mode that supports Unity Catalog.
- In the notebook, create a query that references Unity Catalog tables and views.

To select from a table or view using the SQL Editor:

- In the sidebar, click **SQL Editor**.
- Select a SQL warehouse.
- Compose a query. To insert a table or view into the query, select a catalog and schema, then click the name of the table or view to insert.
- Click **Run**.

To explore data stored in an external location before user creates tables from that data, user can use Data Explorer or the following commands:

```
SELECT * FROM <format>.`abfss://<path-to-files>`;
```

Using Python:
```
display(spark.read.load("abfss://<path-to-files>"))
```

Apply Tags

Tags are attributes containing keys and optional values that user can apply to different securable objects in Unity Catalog. Tagging is useful for organizing and categorizing different securable objects within a metastore. Using tags also simplifies search and discovery of data assets.

Tagging is currently supported on catalogs, schemas, and tables.

To create securable object tags using the Data Explorer UI:

- Click Data in the sidebar.
- Select a securable object to view the tag information.
- Click Add/Edit Tags to manage tags for the current securable object. User can add and remove multiple tags simultaneously in the tag management model.

Work with Unity Catalog and the legacy Hive metastore

If workspace was in service before it was enabled for Unity Catalog, it likely has a Hive metastore that contains data that user wants to continue to use.

The Hive metastore appears as a top-level catalog called hive_metastore in the three-level namespace.

For example, user can refer to a table called sales_detail in the sales schema in the legacy Hive metastore by using the following notation:

SELECT * from hive_metastore.sales.sales_detail;

By using three-level namespace notation, user can join data in a Unity Catalog metastore with data in the legacy Hive metastore.

The following example joins results from the sales_current table in the legacy Hive metastore with the sales_historical table in the Unity Catalog metastore when the order_id fields are equal.

SELECT * FROM hive_metastore.sales.sales_current
JOIN main.shared_sales.sales_historical
ON hive_metastore.sales.sales_current.order_id = main.shared_sales.sales_historical.order_id;

A join with data in the legacy Hive metastore will only work on the workspace where that data resides. Trying to run such a join in another workspace results in an error. Databricks recommends that user upgrades legacy tables and views to Unity Catalog.

Upgrade tables and views to Unity Catalog

Tables in the catalog hive_metastore are registered in the Hive metastore. Any other catalogs listed are governed by Unity Catalog.

To upgrade a table to Unity Catalog as a managed table, use the below command

```
CREATE TABLE <catalog>.<new-schema>.<new-table>
AS SELECT * FROM hive_metastore.<old-schema>.<old-table>;
```

- <catalog>: The Unity Catalog catalog for the new table.
- <new-schema>: The Unity Catalog schema for the new table.
- <new-table>: A name for the Unity Catalog table.
- <old-schema>: The schema for the old table, such as default.
- <old-table>: The name of the old table.

This command creates a managed table in which data is copied into the storage location that was nominated when the metastore was set up.

Databricks SQL

Databricks SQL lets us run all SQL and BI applications at scale with better price and performance.

Create a SQL warehouse

A SQL warehouse is a simplified compute resource that lets us run SQL commands on data objects within Databricks SQL.

Databricks recommends creating a serverless SQL warehouse. Serverless SQL warehouses are fully managed by Azure Databricks and give users instant access to elastic compute resources.

To create a SQL warehouse:
- Click SQL Warehouses in the sidebar then Create SQL Warehouse.
- Enter a Name for the warehouse.
- Accept the default warehouse settings or edit them.
- Click Create.
- The permissions modal appears, where user can give users or groups access to the warehouse.

To grant Databricks SQL access to a user:
- As a workspace admin, go to Admin Settings.
- Click to the Users tab.
- In the user row, click Databricks SQL access.

To manually start a stopped SQL warehouse, click SQL Warehouses in the sidebar then click the start icon next to the warehouse.

To stop a running warehouse, click the stop icon next to the warehouse.

Warehouse settings

Creating a SQL warehouse in the UI requires the following settings:
- *Cluster Size*: Represents the size of the driver node and number of worker nodes associated with the cluster. To reduce query latency, increase the size.
- *Auto Stop*: It determines whether the warehouse stops if it's idle for the specified number of minutes. Idle SQL warehouses continue to accumulate DBU and cloud instance charges until they are stopped.
- *Scaling*: It sets the minimum and maximum number of clusters that will be used for a query. The default is a minimum and a maximum of one cluster. User can increase the maximum clusters if user wants to handle more concurrent users for a given query. Azure Databricks recommends a cluster for every 10 concurrent queries.
- *Type*: It determines the type of warehouse. Databricks SQL supports three warehouse types, each with different levels of performance and feature support.

Warehouse Types

Databricks SQL supports three warehouse types, each with different levels of performance and feature support.

Serverless

Supports all features in the pro SQL warehouse type, as well as advanced Databricks SQL performance features. SQL warehouses run in the customer's Azure Databricks account using serverless compute.

Classic

Supports entry level performance features and a limited set of Databricks SQL functionality.

To upgrade existing SQL warehouses to serverless:
- In the sidebar, click SQL Warehouses.
- In the Actions column, click the vertical ellipsis ⋮ then click *Upgrade to Serverless*.

Pro

Supports additional Databricks SQL performance features (compared to classic) and supports all Databricks SQL functionality.

Monitor a SQL Warehouse

To monitor a SQL warehouse, click the name of a SQL warehouse and then the *Monitoring* tab.

Materialized Views

In Databricks SQL, materialized views are Unity Catalog managed tables that allow users to precompute results based on the latest version of data in source tables. Materialized views reduce cost and improve query latency by pre-computing slow queries and frequently used computations.

Requirements for materialized view are:
- User must use a Unity Catalog-enabled workspace to create and refresh materialized views.
- To create Databricks SQL materialized views user's account must be enabled to use serverless SQL warehouses.

Create a materialized view

To create a materialized view, use the **CREATE MATERIALIZED VIEW** statement. The following example creates the materialized view materialized_view from the base table SalesData:

```
CREATE MATERIALIZED VIEW materialized_view
AS SELECT
 date, sum(sales) AS sum_of_sales
FROM
```

SalesData
GROUP BY
Date

The user who creates a materialized view is the materialized view owner and needs to have the following permissions:

- SELECT privilege on the base tables referenced by the materialized view.
- USE CATALOG and USE SCHEMA privileges on the catalog and schema containing the source tables for the materialized view.
- USE CATALOG and USE SCHEMA privileges on the target catalog and schema for the materialized view.
- CREATE TABLE and CREATE MATERIALIZED VIEW privileges on the schema containing the materialized view.

Refresh a materialized view

The REFRESH operation refreshes the materialized view to reflect the latest changes to the base table. To refresh a materialized view, use the REFRESH MATERIALIZED VIEW statement. Only the owner can REFRESH the materialized view. The following example refreshes the materialized_view materialized view:

REFRESH MATERIALIZED VIEW materialized_view

Schedule materialized view refreshes

User can configure a Databricks SQL materialized view to refresh automatically based on a defined schedule. User can configure this schedule with the SCHEDULE clause when user creates the materialized view or add a schedule with the ALTER VIEW statement.

```
CREATE MATERIALIZED VIEW materialzed_view
  COMMENT 'Daily sales numbers'
  SCHEDULE CRON '0 0 0 * * ? *'
  AS SELECT date AS date, sum(sales) AS sumOfSales
    FROM SalesData
    GROUP BY date;
```

The materialized view created above will be refreshed daily at midnight.

Drop a materialized view

To drop a materialized view, use the DROP VIEW statement. The following example drops the materialized_view materialized view:

DROP MATERIALIZED VIEW materialized_view

A materialized view owner can grant **SELECT** privileges to other users. Users with **SELECT** access to the materialized view do not need **SELECT** access to the tables referenced by the materialized view.

To grant access to a materialized view, use the GRANT statement:

```
GRANT
  privilege_type [, privilege_type ] ...
  ON <mv_name> TO principal
```

The following example creates a materialized view and grants select privileges to a user:

```
CREATE MATERIALIZED VIEW <mv_name> AS SELECT FROM <base_table>
GRANT SELECT ON <mv_name> TO user
```

Revoke privileges from a materialized view

To revoke access from a materialized view, use the REVOKE statement.

```
REVOKE
  privilege_type [, privilege_type ]
  ON <name> FROM principal
```

When SELECT privileges on a base table are revoked from the materialized view owner or any other user who has been granted SELECT privileges to the materialized view, the materialized view owner or user granted access is still able to query the materialized view. However, the following behaviour occurs:

- The materialized view owner or others who have lost access to a materialized view can no longer REFRESH that materialized view, and the materialized view will become stale.
- If automated with a schedule, the next scheduled REFRESH fails or is not run.

The following example revokes the SELECT privilege from `materialized_view`.

```
REVOKE SELECT ON materialized_view FROM user1;
```

Materialized views always return the latest snapshot version of data available in base tables at the time of the last refresh. Materialized view can be incrementally refreshed or sometimes it may be full refresh as well.

Materialized view is incrementally refreshed in case of the following conditions.

- The materialized view can query only a single table or perform an INNER JOIN and UNION ALL (or combinations of INNER JOIN and UNION ALL) on multiple tables.
- The materialized view must have a GROUP BY in the main select clause.
- The materialized view SELECT clause supports the following aggregate functions. Any aggregate function not in this list is not supported:
  - SUM
  - COUNT

Incremental refresh is not supported for materialized views that include:
- Window functions.
- HAVING clauses.
- Subqueries in SELECT or WHERE clauses.

Materialized views cannot be created using the Delta Lake time travel feature. LEFT JOINs and OUTER JOINs are not supported.

Change data feed is not enabled by default on materialized views. To enable the change data feed on a materialized view, specify the appropriate table setting at creation time. If user have an existing materialized view, user must drop it and re-create it.

The following example enables change data feed on a materialized view:

CREATE MATERIALIZED VIEW <mv_name> TBLPROPERTIES (delta.enableChangeDataFeed = true) AS SELECT FROM <base_table>

To optimize the performance of materialized view refreshes, Databricks uses a cost model to select the technique used for the refresh. The following table describes these techniques:

Technique	Incremental refresh?	Description
FULL_RECOMPUTE	No	The materialized view was fully recomputed
NO_OP	Not applicable	The materialized view was not updated because no changes to the base table were detected.
ROW_BASED or PARTITION_OVERWRITE	Yes	The materialized view was incrementally refreshed using the specified technique.

Materialized views do not support identity columns or surrogate keys. User cannot run ad hoc OPTIMIZE or VACUUM commands against materialized views.